SECOND EDITION

A Junior High School Music Handbook

SALLY MONSOUR
Professor, College of Music
University of Colorado, Boulder

MARGARET PERRY
Vocal Music Teacher
Doolen Junior High School, Tucson

Prentice-Hall, Inc., Englewood Cliffs, New Jersey

Printed in the United States of America

13–512467–0

Library of Congress Catalog Card Number: 74–79832

Current printing (last digit):
10 9 8 7 6 5 4 3 2 1

PRENTICE-HALL INTERNATIONAL, INC., London
PRENTICE-HALL OF AUSTRALIA, PTY. LTD., Sydney
PRENTICE-HALL OF CANADA, LTD., Toronto
PRENTICE HALL OF INDIA PRIVATE LTD., New Delhi
PRENTICE-HALL OF JAPAN, INC., Tokyo

Foreword

There are at least two ways of evaluating a book:

1. Do the *authors* know what they're writing about—through first-hand experience? Sally Monsour and Margaret Perry do. I know them both personally. They have conducted workshops and teaching seminars for teachers. They are master teachers, proven in the tempering fires of the junior high school classroom with immense success.

2. Does the *content* meet the *need*? This book does. Every junior high school vocal teacher, experienced or not, feels the need for ideas, assistance in organization, suggestions for improvement, sure-fire lesson plans, and new approaches to old problems.

This book offers:
a. up-dated references and sources of supply.
b. lessons using contemporary music completely integrated into each chapter.
c. a new and valuable chapter on tone color in music.
d. lessons in miniature . . . take-off points for further exploration.

As a practicing music administrator, I provide this book for each of my junior high school vocal instructors. It provides a ready reference that is inspirational, practical, and more constantly available than I could ever be personally. It is positively the finest thing of its kind in print. I recommend it without reservation for teachers-in-the-making, as well as for teachers in the classroom.

Dr. Max T. Ervin
Director of Music Education
Tucson, Arizona

v

Preface

The title—*A Junior High School Music Handbook*—best describes the contents and purposes this book. From beginning to end, it is meant to be a practical guide for the present and future music teachers of students in their early teen years.

In this second edition, a special effort has been made to update learning concepts and teaching procedures. The availability of new teaching aids has also accounted for the alteration of references to current music texts and recordings for the junior high level.

The suggested lessons and procedures have been tested in actual teaching situations. For the most part, the recordings and song materials are taken from the standard music repertory. Furthermore, a deliberate attempt has been made to avoid lengthy theoretical or philosophical explanations in favor of brief, concise statements and directions.

By means of the organization and content, the authors make a direct appeal on behalf of a musically-oriented approach to classroom music. The sections on understanding melody, rhythm, harmony, tone color, and form are the result of lengthy discussions with teachers who have expressed concern over the teaching of lasting musical values through the study of musical elements, especially at the junior high school level. But because of the ever-present necessity for aural communication in music, the experiences of singing, of listening, or of playing instruments have been integrated into every lesson on the elements of music.

Since teenagers enter the music class with vast individual differences in physical characteristics, school and community backgrounds, and attitudes toward music, the teacher must be alert to the many imaginative ways of presenting music during this age span.

In general, the contents of this book are a result of the teaching experiences of the authors in both colleges and public schools. In addition, many colleagues in the field have graciously contributed teaching ideas and suggestions.

Sally Monsour
Margaret Perry

Contents

7

Understanding Harmony   **72**

8

Understanding Tone Color   **83**

9

Understanding Form   **91**

10

Relating Content   **99**

Appendix A:

The Music Classroom   **107**

1

The Music Class
in the Junior High School

"Our primary concern should be to consider the essential nature of music as an art in formulating our objectives in terms of children's expected musical behavior . . . we should expect that from the very beginning there are vitally interesting and significant musical meanings which children should learn in their own terms." (GLADYS TIPTON, Music Educators Journal)

"To the degree that one is able to approach learning as a task of discovering something rather than 'learning about' it, to that degree will be a tendency for the child to carry out his learning activities with the autonomy of self-reward, or, more properly, by reward that is discovery itself." (JEROME BRUNER, The Process of Education)

"Our first duty is to the children of America, to keep before them life's finest ideals and the highest standards of human conduct, to give every child the loving attention we should like children of our own to receive from their teachers, to raise them up in the spirit of and practice of human brotherhood. Our second duty is to the art of music, one of the most glorious products of the human mind and spirit. To strive for the highest excellence in this art is to do the most honor to our best natures, for we are never so human as when we forget our petty and personal concerns in the contemplation of truth and beauty." (ALLEN P. BRITTON, Music Educators Journal)

Objectives

The objectives of the music class in the junior high school may be listed as follows:

— to provide students with the means for understanding and enjoying music

— to provide students with the means for continuing progress toward the refinement of musical taste

— to provide rewarding experiences for making music regardless of the individual differences of students

— to provide students with a musical repertory that has gained significance in their musical heritage

— to provide the talented and creative students with the encouragement to pursue musical excellence

— to provide experiences through which students will develop the capacity for self-expression

— to provide students with the means for the rewarding use of leisure time

— to provide situations through which students will develop habits of individual responsibility and group concern

Scheduling the Music Class

Since art and music are so fundamental to full and satisfactory living at all levels of civilization, need we belabor the argument that they must be given a place not only in the elective areas of the curriculum but also as part of the common learnings. (F. E. Engleman, Executive Secretary, American Association of School Administrators)

Grades 7 through 9 are usually incorporated into one of three distinct types of school organization:

1. an eight-grade elementary school (8–4)
2. a separate junior high school (6–3–3), (6–2–4)
3. a six-grade secondary school (6–6)

It is recognized that music may be taught effectively within a variety of scheduling plans. Some type of musical opportunity must be required for *all* students. However, those with above-average musical ability or interest must be given the opportunity to elect a performing group (band, orchestra, choir), as well as a general music class.

Directly linked to both scheduling and learning objectives is the question of general music class size. When the size exceeds that of a regular academic class, the purposes of general music are often defeated. As a result, teachers resort to "group" activities, such as passive listening, film viewing, or recreational singing. Little or no individual expression or participation occurs. In addition, severe discipline problems become more frequent.

The following are examples of existing scheduling patterns.

— The class meets every day for approximately nine weeks of the semester; during the other nine-week period, students enroll in art, shop, etc.

— The class meets three days one week and two the next for the entire semester, usually alternating with art.

— The class meets one or two days per week for the entire year.

— The class is incorporated into one of several varieties of flexible scheduling.[1]

Also related to scheduling is the length of time for class periods. In this regard, there seems to be considerable variety, especially in flexible scheduling situations. It should be noted, however, that the exclusive scheduling of too-short or too-long periods is not desirable.

REMEMBER   Sometimes it is the responsibility of the music department to initiate imaginative suggestions for scheduling. These should take into account the specific nature of music and the overall needs and facilities of the entire school.

The Students

In general, early adolescent students may be characterized by the following personality traits:

— energetic—need active participation

— fluctuate from excitement to depression—need understanding

— desire to cast off the "old-fashioned" and to be "modern" and "in style," limitations which are often short-lived—need guidance

— love excitement and adventure—need variety

— exhibit sharp changes in interests and attitudes—need stability

— desire status as individuals—need encouragement and social acceptance

Adolescents may exhibit a polarity of reactions to both the music class and its teacher. These students have the capacity for being highly enthusiastic in a situation which provides stimulation, variety, and an atmosphere for learning. Without these provisions, however, the same students will often react with varying amounts of indifference, belligerence, or even rudeness. These reactions must be accommodated realistically.

Many students feel free in expressing their attitudes, and the following comment was written by a seventh-grade boy.

"Music is the most worthy, courteous, pleasant, and joyous, and lovely of all knowledge; it makes a man gentlemanly in his demeanor . . . for it acts upon his feelings. Music encourages us to bear the heaviest of afflictions, administers consolation in every difficulty, refreshes the broken spirit, removes headache, and cures crossness and melancholy."

I got this little saying out of *The Heritage of Music* (Shippen, Katherine B.,

[1]For reference on flexible scheduling, *see* Donald Manlove and David Beggs III, *Bold New Ventures* (Bloomington, Ind.: Indiana University Press, 1965).

and Anca Seidlova, Viking, 1963). I just wanted you to know that this is the way I feel about music. I may not know my notes so well—but I am sure willing to learn . . . *Don, 7th Grade.*

The following essay reflects the attitude of a ninth-grade student who was considering music as a career.

I WANT TO BE A MUSIC TEACHER

A musician who teaches music in the schools may help children to develop their talents. The teacher may also arouse an interest and a love for music in the pupils and help them to enjoy making music for others.

If a teacher really has an interest in her music, she will get a deep satisfaction from it. It is also a challenge to help a student or a group of students with something and help them perfect it. This takes time but it is gratifying in the end.

To become a music teacher, whether public school or private, takes lots of hard work and study. One also has to keep up her study so she can keep up with the latest methods, etc. Sometimes one has to travel from her home to distant cities to get the training she wants or needs.

If a person is really a good musician, she will be in demand by the community in which she lives. She may find it hard to keep up with all the demands of the public.

After working hard with her students in order to give a program, a teacher is rewarded because she knows the program was well done. It must be a great satisfaction to know that one has done a job well. . . . It should give one a good feeling to realize that she has brought enjoyment to others and perhaps helped them to like music better.

PHYSICAL CHARACTERISTICS

Puberty for both boys and girls usually occurs soon after the largest increase in height and weight. Regardless of what the average age for this occurrence may be, individual differences exist. Some girls, for example, may reach their maximum growth period as early as 12 years and some boys as late as 15.

Most students entering the adolescent period exhibit the following physical characteristics:

— awkwardness and lack of detailed coordination resulting from rapid muscle and bone growth
— restlessness, nervousness, and headaches (sometimes imaginary) resulting from glandular changes and adjustments
— changes in range and quality of voice resulting from lengthening of vocal cords
— shyness and sensitivity sometimes resulting from skin disorders

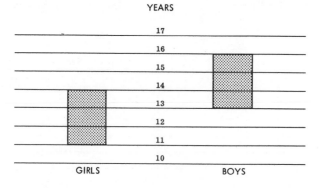

Period of greatest height-weight growth rate.

READINESS AND BACKGROUND

Students enter the junior high school with varying amounts of readiness and background for the activities of the music class. The extremes may be wide and often exist within the same class. Here are a few examples:

— enthusiasm for music of good quality	vs.	— negative attitude toward most music
— healthy attitude about music in the home	vs.	— practically no musical opportunities in the home
— private or class instrumental instruction for several years	vs.	— no previous instrumental experience
— extensive and proper use of the singing voice	vs.	— poor singing habits
— vocal independence and proficiency in sight reading	vs.	— random information about notation
— few coordinative problems	vs.	— extreme coordinative problems
— familiarity with classroom instruments	vs.	— no knowledge of classroom instruments

COMMUNITY

The standards, expectations and pressures of the community will tend to influence the students' reactions to music. They should be taken into account when planning the content of the class and when evaluating progress.

Some community characteristics that may affect the students' attitudes toward music are:

		CUMULATIVE RECORD		
	Name			Year of birth
Grade	Activity	Special Abilities	Comments	School and teacher
4				
5				
6				
7				
8				
9				
10				
11				
12				

ANECDOTAL RECORD

Name	Age
Class	Date

— stable or shifting population

— urban, suburban, or rural community

— conservative or liberal philosophy

— rich, poor, or average culture

REMEMBER Students enter the music class the first day—boys and girls, pre-adolescents and adolescents, tall and short, skinny and chubby, painfully shy and "painfully" aggressive. They also enter with a wide diversity of musical capacity, accomplishment, and experience—from the "I just love music" attitude to "Music is for the birds!"

GETTING TO KNOW THE STUDENTS

There are many ways of getting acquainted with the students and becoming familiar with their backgrounds at the beginning of the term.

— Ask students about themselves.
— Find out what they expect from the music class.
— Observe them outside of the classroom.
— Talk to their parents and other teachers.
— Utilize a recording device such as an anecdotal record, questionnaire, inventory, cumulative record, survey test, or information card.

As an example of the use of a questionnaire or information card, the following replies were received in response to the question: "What do you expect in junior high music?"

"Leaving knowing more than I did when I came in."
"Sing unusual songs and learn their history."
"I would expect the singing would be more difficult—more parts."
"In the seventh grade, I'd expect to learn more about music."
"I would like for this class to be one of my best ones."
"I don't know—I never had school music."
"I think we will read of musicians and learn what their great art was."
"I don't expect to sing because I came from a long line of monotones."
"Being taught how to sing and the basic parts of music."
"Go deeply into studying music in other countries, such as instruments played, music done, and composers."
"Foke music (sic!)."

REMEMBER   Human development and behavior are so complex that the wise teacher will reserve judgment regarding the responses and attitudes of students in any specific situation. An understanding of any *single* factor hardly enables the teacher to predict with any degree of certainty how a student will respond in a future situation. For this reason, it is important to gather as much information from as many sources as possible in order to gain a consistent knowledge of the students and their behavior patterns.

EVALUATION OF STUDENTS

The primary factor in evaluation is the extent to which the student develops an understanding of music. Such an accomplishment should be viewed in terms of the student's ability.

However, the very nature of music makes the evaluation of students in the music class very difficult. Musical understanding deals with many intangible factors that cannot be tested with traditional objective devices.

If one letter or numerical grade is given, it should represent the *total* picture of the student's achievement in the class. However, a grade for *each* of the following might reflect his accomplishment more accurately. (In the case of special projects, the teacher may wish to assign extra credit.)

— attitude
— effort
— cooperation
— participation in class activities
— musical achievement toward the established goals of the class
— contribution to the class as a whole

SPECIAL PROJECTS

— Prepare and present an oral book report to the class.[2]
— Write a review of a concert, stage production, recommended movie, TV show, or radio program.
— Prepare a musical notebook.
— Prepare a bulletin board.
— Contribute newspaper and magazine articles of musical interest.
— Alert other class members to coming musical events in the community, on radio and TV.
— Perform for the class (piano, vocal solo, etc.).
— Illustrate a song sung in class.
— Illustrate a composition listened to in class.
— Prepare an accompaniment for a song performed in class (autoharp, piano, ukulele, guitar, rhythm instrument, etc.).
— Bring in a favorite record "worthy of our class time"; tell why it is a favorite; tell something about the record that will increase the listening enjoyment of the class.
— Make an instrument which can be used in class.
— Prepare an oral report on a favorite composer or instrument.

In order to evaluate the quality and merit of special projects, the teacher may wish to establish a point system.

When grades are given:

— be sure that students, parents, and administrators know the basis upon which grades are given

[2]The school library should have an adequate supply of books about music. See Appendix G, page 130, for a list of suggested books for the school library.

— help the student to be aware of the particular areas in which he is making the most progress

— be consistent

— always be ready to justify the grade given to a student

— help the student understand what he can do to improve his grade

Consistency within an organized framework is important in evaluation. Neglect of this fact often makes students indifferent toward music and music grading. Note the attitude reflected in the following comments.

HOW TO GET AN "A" IN MUSIC CLASS
(As analyzed by an eighth-grade boy)

You smile at the teacher.

You laugh at the corny jokes.

You tell him how you like the record, even if you don't.

You go up after class and ask him a question.

You tell him you heard the record he played on the radio last night.

You go in after school and help him clean up the place.

Pretend you are always singing even if you only make your mouth move.

You don't tell the teacher he is wrong, even if you know he is.

You try to keep your hands in your pocket and your feet on the floor and don't look at anyone else.

And even if you do all this you won't have a very good chance because you aren't a girl!

REMEMBER   Musical talent is often closely related to achievement, interest, and contribution to the class. Although a single grade should not be determined by musical talent alone, it is important to consider a student's achievement based upon his capacity. There will also be many students with minimal ability. Their grades should be partially determined by factors which are essentially nonmusical in nature.

The Teacher

COMPETENCIES

The members of any single profession share certain techniques, knowledge, and information in common. The following list includes those desirable competencies which (1) all teachers, (2) all music teachers, and (3) all junior high general music teachers should share.

All competent teachers should:

— know the facts of physical, emotional, social, and intellectual development

— gain a mastery of the psychological data basic to an understanding of the many facets of human learning

— integrate the isolated facts of human development into a substantial framework of knowledge

— make a healthy adjustment to their own problems of living

— possess a general understanding and sympathy for all academic disciplines

All competent music teachers should:

— have personal conviction regarding the role of music in the school and in the culture

— love music and appreciate its unique value in human living

— possess an artistic understanding of musical styles and periods, proficiency regarding the theoretical aspects of a score (including functional keyboard and sight singing), ability to perform acceptably on at least one musical instrument, ability to conduct clearly and expressively

— know the musical backgrounds, interests, attitudes, and abilities of the students

— know the most effective methods for helping each student achieve maximum *musical* understanding

— possess skill in detecting and diagnosing musical problems

All competent junior high general music teachers should:

— possess specific knowledge of the adolescent and an unlimited quantity of enthusiasm regarding his needs

— possess a working framework regarding the characteristics of the changing voice

— have the ability to arrange simple songs for various vocal ranges, and to rearrange and orchestrate a score quickly and easily

— possess a somewhat detailed knowledge of composers, styles, and forms

— possess sufficient pianistic facility to accompany songs, improvise accompaniments, and transpose simple songs at sight

— have considerable knowledge of orchestral and band instruments—their development, and their function

REMEMBER   Because of individual differences, the amount and nature of these characteristics will naturally vary among members of the teaching profession.

ATTITUDES AND REACTIONS

There are times when some junior high music teachers complain: "The reason I can't teach them anything is because they didn't learn anything in grade school!"; "If *they* would only teach these students to read music, my job would be simple!"; "I wouldn't be so concerned about general music if they just had a receptive attitude!"; "It's my job to adjust to *them*, why can't they adjust to *me*?"; "Is my primary concern the training of singers for the high school choir?"

These complaints sometimes stem from situations over which the teacher has little control. On the other hand, many situations may be improved by giving special attention to the following list of *Dos* and *Don'ts*.

DO

— Be aware of what good quality in music means.

— Try constantly to improve your own musicianship.

— Maintain your own enthusiasm for music.

— Become acquainted with music that is new and challenging to you as a mature musician.

— Be aware of music that is *really* too difficult for your students.

— Believe that adolescents can learn to sing accurately and artistically.

— Be willing to treat all music with an element of respect and tolerance.

— Plan your lessons with a purpose.

— Encourage curiosity in the musical phases of instruction.

— Assure your students that you know and understand their problems.

— Set a wholesome example for the class by your appearance.

— Explore new teaching materials and techniques.

— Understand and appreciate adolescent humor.

— Enjoy the anticipation of a new or unexpected reaction from the class. (Some of your most exciting lessons will occur spontaneously.)

— Encourage musical and verbal self-expression.

— Take verbal explanations and comments of students seriously.

DON'T

— Think of yourself as a singer, pianist, or choral director, but as a *musician* and *teacher*.

— Inform students of your own peculiar prejudice or bias—musical or otherwise.

— Ignore or ridicule student standards of music—their likes or dislikes. (A wise teacher will take note of these and plan accordingly.)

— Praise *everything* all the time. (Be discriminating and honest but always keep in mind the needs and capacities of both the individual and the group.)

— Be critical of other teachers when talking to students—not even by implication.

— Try to over-impress the students with your lofty knowledge or brilliant vocabulary.

— Falsify your personality.

— Inject answers to questions in questions themselves.

— Hesitate to admit your errors. (Students are quick to recognize a teacher who is bluffing.)

— Assume that the popular teacher has to be "one of the kids."

REMEMBER Confidence, poise, and security in front of the class depend largely upon being well prepared.

The Teacher and the Class

"The teacher can shut his eyes to the psyche system of the classroom, but he cannot make it disappear." (Herbert Thelen, Professor of Education, University of Chicago)

MOTIVATION

The make-up of the group and the method of the teacher stand side by side in affecting the quality of the educational process. Obviously, every group contains a variety of motivational forces which will determine individual productivity. For this reason, it seems that a teaching approach should allow individual inquiry and freedom to discover relationships. This would result in a higher calibre of qualitative response than a drillmaster approach, even though the latter might result in a reasonable mastery of content.

The list below indicates the polarity of motivational factors which generate group as well as individual learning. A realistic appraisal of these factors and their interaction in the classroom should be made by all teachers.

↑ beauty of the music
evidence of musical achievement
anticipated success
specific rewards
emulation of a model
acceptance by the group
approval by the teacher
social prestige
competition
threat of failure
force of authority
fear of punishment

The following are several points of departure for motivating students. The specific lesson will determine which motivations are appropriate.

— Inspire students to reflect upon questions of musical value, i.e., "Why is the following considered a masterwork?" "Why is this song a part of our heritage?"

— Use anecdotes related to the composition, composer, conductor, first performance, special recording, exceptional artists, etc.

— Suggest student projection into the role of composer or arranger.

— Play a good recording of the song to be learned. This may include performances by former students.

— Discuss interesting aspects of the text and its relationship to the music.

— Relate personal experiences that you or others have had with the music.

— Inspire the students with the anticipation of a forthcoming event in which the class will perform for the enjoyment of others.

— When appropriate, utilize out-of-class experiences such as current movies, TV programs, or local performances.

GROUP PROCESSES[3]

Whether or not students will inquire into musical meanings and express themselves in the musical language will depend somewhat upon the role of the teacher in the classroom. For example, the teacher may assume (1) an autocratic role by controlling all decisions, (2) the role of a follower by allowing the students to control all decisions, or (3) the role of a guide by providing the necessary leadership to enable students to inquire and discover for themselves.

Teaching Suggestions

The following suggestions and sample questions point up several practical considerations of a teaching approach in which the stimulation of student discovery is the primary aim.

— Encourage vocal and rhythmic responses as well as verbal explanations and answers.

— Derive extra-musical ideas from the musical elements of the composition.

— Utilize comparison and contrast such as a transcription with the original, an art song executed by various voice types, or a simple and a sophisticated rendition of the same folk song.

— Derive from the musical sound as often as possible musical facts concerning composer, style, or period.

— Repeat familiar compositions with altered emphasis or attention to increasingly greater complexities.

— Repeat familiar musical forms in unfamiliar compositions.

— Emphasize that the concepts "what to listen *to*" and "what to listen *for*" complement rather than oppose each other.

— Attempt to use colorful yet accurate words to describe the sound.

[3]For an excellent treatment of group responses and inquiry as learning processes see Herbert A. Thelen, *Education and the Human Quest* (New York: Harper & Row, Publishers, 1960), pp. 113–159.

Teacher-directed classroom.

Student-directed classroom.

Teacher guides;
students discover.

(Drawings by Carol Wagoner, Ninth-grade student)

FORMULA FOR PREVENTIVE DISCIPLINE AND CLASSROOM MANAGEMENT

Create an atmosphere in which getting down to business seems the natural way of behaving. (*C. P. Smith*)

Problems of discipline usually arise because the teacher (1) is unable to plan an interesting or effective lesson, (2) does not enjoy students of junior high school age, (3) lacks knowledge regarding the musical capabilities and problems of adolescents, (4) must handle too large a class. The following are suggestions which will tend to create a wholesome classroom atmosphere and divert many discipline problems.

In general:

- Know your subject. Students will usually respect this qualification.
- Show by your attitude that you expect desirable behavior.
- Have all routine matters well organized so that students can direct their attention to the lesson at hand.
- Allow freedom within stipulated boundaries of control.
- Be interes*ting* and interested.
- Don't make mountains out of molehills.
- Be firm, fair, and friendly.
- Be consistent and practice self-control. Don't blow your top.

— Make sure students are accomplishing something and are aware of their success.

— Plan lessons in which the majority will be interested.

— Plan varied lessons involving active participation.

— Don't allow a few students to monopolize class discussions.

— Don't neglect the shy or indifferent student because your attention is continually diverted by the outgoing or eager.

— Keep your voice clear, confident, and well-modulated. Speak quietly and personally to an offender.

— Avoid monotonous or distracting mannerisms.

— Avoid the habit of calling on the office for solutions to troublesome behavior.

— Don't show favoritism. If you can't help it, hide it.

— Don't talk down to students.

— Don't do things in the classroom you have told students not to do.

— Set an example by being courteous toward *all* students, teachers, and administrative personnel.

Specifically:

— Exhibit considerable leadership the first few weeks.

— Be in the room or at the door when students enter.

— Have students go directly to their seats when the class begins.

— Designate individuals to distribute materials to class members in an orderly fashion.

— Have papers arranged by rows before distributing them.

— Make individual assignments in order to challenge certain class members.

— Don't talk to the blackboard.

— Encourage a troublesome student to discuss and analyze (privately) his actions in relation to classroom behavior.

— Remember that a mere 30- to 60-minute penalty of staying after school seldom solves any problem.

RELATIONSHIPS WITH THE SCHOOL STAFF

It is important that the music teacher maintain a good working relationship with the school administration and other members of the staff.

— Familiarize yourself with the other programs in the school—Mathematics, English, Physical Education, etc.

— Attend faculty meetings regularly.

— Volunteer your services in the formulation of school policies and procedures. This does not necessitate forcing your opinions on others.

— Accept assignments cheerfully. Other staff members are also busy.

— Make yourself a member of the school team. Call on key teachers, counselors, and administrators for help when *really* needed.

— Be prompt. Arrive on time, get reports to the office when due, report your grades by the deadline.

— Make all office announcements to your class when requested.

The music teacher joins other members of the school staff in the formulation of school policy.

— Cooperate with other teachers at every opportunity.

— Share the responsibility for *general* school discipline.

— Take an active interest in all school functions and activities.

— Go to your next P.T.A. meeting. Remember, *you are the "T" in the P.T.A.*

REMEMBER The students, the teachers, the school staff, and the parents make up the human element which affects the significant phases of any learning situation. The music class is no exception. The successful music teacher should always be aware that music is one area of a broad curriculum. When this is made evident, other members of the staff are usually ready to accept the music teacher as an important member of the entire teaching profession.

OFF TO A GOOD START!

To a large degree, the success of the music class will depend upon your initial contact with the students. Prepare the first day's plan carefully. A suggested plan is given below. It assumes a new teacher in a new situation.

The First Day:

— 1. Introduce yourself—write your name on the board.

— 2. Sing a few familiar songs such as "Battle Hymn of the Republic," "America the Beautiful," "Camptown Races."

— 3. Teach a new song. The following rounds are possibilities:

Make New Friends[4]

Tune from Cooperative Recreation Service. Used by permission.

How Good It Is My Brothers

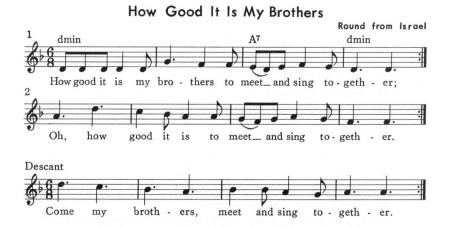

From *Holiday Songs*, Carroll Rinehart and Alan Mills, Bowmar Records, Inc., 1966.

— 4. "I am anxious to become acquainted with you." Students fill out 4 x 6 information cards.

— 5. Play an appropriate recording such as "Getting to Know You" from *The King and I.*

[4]Poem "New Friends and Old Friends" from which the words of this song were taken was written by Joseph Parry, *Best Loved Poems of American People*, selected by Hazel Felleman (New York: Doubleday, 1936).

INFORMATION CARD

Name _____ Age _____ Grade _____   Class Period _____

Address _____ Tel. No. ._____

Which school did you attend last year? _____

In what musical organizations did you participate --- band, orchestra, chorus,

church choir, etc.? _____

Which musical instrument(s) do you play, if any?   _____

Which of the following do you have in your home? --- radio, T.V.,

phonograph, piano, tape recorder, other.   _____

_____

What kind of songs do you like to sing?   _____

What kind of music do you like to listen to?   _____

What do you expect in junior high music?   _____

_____

Seat Number _____

This card may be used to record results of voice testing, to transfer names to seating chart, and to alphabetize and record names in grade book.

— 6. Sing another familiar song.
— 7. Dismiss the class in an orderly fashion.

The Second Day:

— 1. Check roll from cards prepared the first day.
— 2. Sing a few familiar songs.
— 3. Review one of the songs learned the previous day.
— 4. Add other parts with instruments and/or voices. (See below)
— 5. Introduce a new song with the books. If possible, select one for which there is an interesting recording.
— 6. Sing another familiar song, preferably one that is currently popular.
— 7. Dismiss class in an orderly fashion.

Make   new   friends.   Make   new   friends.   etc.

CLASSROOM ORGANIZATION

As soon as possible establish classroom routines such as roll taking, distribution and collection of materials, and dismissal of the class. The following are procedures that experienced teachers have followed.

- On the first day, take the roll by having paper prepared with row 1, seat 1, etc. Place one paper in each row. Students sign names as they are singing. By the second day have a *temporary* seating chart prepared. Check the roll as each student pronounces his name and seat number. Assign a student-secretary to accept the responsibility for roll taking.

- On the board, list names of books for the day as a cue for distributing materials by row captains or librarians. If no materials are to be used, indicate this on the board. For variety, prepare a few questions for the students to ponder while books and materials are being distributed.

- Allow a class monitor or chairman to dismiss the students. Rotate this job every few weeks.

- Set the stage for subsequent days by keeping the following in mind during the first few class meetings:
  - Let the students get some insight into your musical expectations for them.
  - Be enthusiastic about their class.
  - Establish a contact that will engender respect and a willingness to cooperate.
  - Refrain from spending most of any one class period on organizational detail.

REMEMBER   This is a music class, so let the music begin.

2

Singing

Will singing prove to be interesting, embarrassing, or dismal for your students? Will you select songs, which represent a wide range of interest? Will you encourage the students in their efforts? Will you know the individual voices in the class? Will you sing songs within the students' vocal ranges and technical abilities? Will you help the student understand that his vocal problems are shared by others in the class? Will your students feel free to discuss their vocal problems with you?

Junior high school students should experience many rewards from a well-rounded singing program. Such a program should include songs of recreational value as well as songs of high artistic value. Recreational songs are those which usually have immediate melodic or rhythmic appeal. They possess a folk quality easily associated with human experiences and events, community or national pride, and so forth. Songs of this type are not usually studied with a view to performance. They are, however, an essential part of the singing program because of their significant place in our common musical heritage.

Songs of high art value are also important to a well-balanced singing program. Songs in this category are usually composed and require study and practice for accurate and artistic execution. They are usually heard in performance rather than in recreational or amateur situations. The schools have a special obligation to acquaint students with songs of this type. If the factors of motivation and voice range are accounted for, students will usually find experiences with this music stimulating and rewarding. Students possessing a high level of ability and achievement will, of course, find particular satisfaction from the study of artistic music, through singing and listening. However, in later life both musical consumers and producers will profit from a singing program which includes both recreational songs and songs of high art value.

Uses in Later Life

There are many lasting values to be derived from a satisfying singing program in school.

CONSUMERS

- aesthetic enjoyment
- appreciation of vocal and instrumental music through listening to concerts, radio, and recordings
- community singing—service clubs, church, etc.
- home—family
- sing along with phonograph, radio, TV
- appreciate the music program in schools

PRODUCERS

- aesthetic enjoyment
- appreciation of vocal and instrumental music through listening to concerts, radio, and recordings
- community choruses performing masterworks
- church choirs
- lead singing in service clubs, scouts, etc.
- home—family (usually harmonize)
- encourage a school music program which includes participation

REMEMBER   When selecting song material, the degree of difficulty is not always predicated upon tonal or metric complexity. For example, visually complex patterns are often easy because of their musical feeling. On the other hand, some passages which appear simple in notation are difficult because they are lacking in musical expression.

Voices

CLASSIFICATIONS

Because the individual development of adolescents does not follow a consistent pattern, the voices of junior high students are varied in range. Consequently, there will be three general categories of voices in the music classes: unchanged, changing, and changed. Within these categories, ranges will vary considerably.[1]

Girl and Boy Sopranos
Although the range remains high, qualities of breathiness and some huskiness appear as the change takes place. Boy sopranos tend to acquire a more brilliant quality at the point of change.

Girl and Boy Altos
Although lower in range than the soprano, it lacks the characteristic resonance of the mature alto.

Alto-Tenors or Cambiata
Although usually limited in range, these few tones tend to be quite resonant in quality. (Alto–Tenors and cambiatas are designations for the changing voice).

Baritones or Basses
Although low in range, the quality will at first lack fullness and roundness.

Voice Testing

In order to insure that students will be singing within a comfortable range, the teacher must establish some type of testing procedure. The group procedure below has been widely used by many teachers. However, it is suggested that voice testing be delayed until the students feel familiar in the class situation.

[1]See Appendix B page 111, for part-songs which fit the above classifications.

GENERAL CONSIDERATIONS

When testing voices keeping these fundamentals in mind.

— See that students understand the purpose of voice testing.

— Discuss briefly the interesting changes taking place in their voices.

— Have the entire class sing the melodies to be used for testing.

— Organize the voice testing procedure efficiently.

— If necessary, sing along with the shy student.

— Encourage students to request a voice check when their assigned parts feel out of range.

GROUP PROCEDURE

Group testing is an effective way to discover the range limits of student voices in a general music class. This is especially so when groups are large. It is also important when students are unfamiliar with the school, the teacher, and their classmates.

During the course of the year, it is sometimes necessary to test voices individually. Students may request voice testing or the teacher may wish to know the specific nature of individual student voices in the group. Furthermore, individual testing is important for auditioning choir and ensemble members.

1. Class sings through "America" in a key of G major (selection to be used in testing). Teacher plays melody in octaves.
2. Class sings first phrase (range of a 5th).
3. Choose a row or small group (not more than 8–10 students) to sing the first phrase while the teacher listens in close proximity to the group.
4. Boys who sing an octave lower are assigned temporarily to a changing voice category.
5. With the same group, repeat the phrase in the key of B-flat major. Those who sing the upper octave range easily are designated as sopranos. Remaining are assigned as altos.
6. Continue above procedure until the entire class has been tested and assigned to either the soprano, alto, or changing voice category.
7. Proceed by testing the changing voices to determine those students who may be baritones. Use a similar group procedure having students sing the first phrase of "America" in the key of C major. Give starting pitches in octaves. Those who sing easily in the lower octave range are assigned as baritones.

In the seventh grade, the last step in the procedure above may not be necessary. A boy's speaking voice and physical characteristics will be clues as to whether the procedure is required.

REMEMBER   As voices begin to change it is essential to introduce harmony parts which will accommodate the resulting limitations in range.

SEATING ARRANGEMENTS

The seating arrangement you select will probably depend on (1) the physical characteristics of the room itself, (2) the number of pupils on each part, and (3) the number of independent singers. Following are suggestions for seating arrangements which have been used successfully.

In many seventh-grade classes the altos are the lowest singers.

Altos and alto-tenors can easily sing together on some harmony songs.

It is often easier for basses to carry their own part when they are on the outside. Alto-tenors are far enough away from the sopranos to avoid the temptation of doubling their part an octave lower.

If the bass section is strong, it is sometimes advantageous to place them near the sopranos.

The changing and changed voices are near the front.

Good Classroom Singing

Although the content of the general music class is not primarily aimed toward the development of professional singers, group singing experiences for most students will be enriched by attention to artistic singing.

The students should sing many songs and themes which are intended primarily to enrich other aspects of the music program. At the same time, there will be many selections presented for their enduring vocal qualities. These will often serve as vehicles for developing an appreciation of singing.

Good classroom singing results from many factors. The purpose of the particular song being studied will determine the extent to which these factors are emphasized. The following are among the aspects of good classroom singing.

— practice of correct posture

— support of the tone by the proper amount and even flow of air

— open throat and relaxed jaw

— accurate intervals within a part

— aural awareness of individual parts in relation to the entire musical context, especially the harmony

— proper enunciation of words

— uniformity of vowel sounds and placement of consonants for rhythmic accuracy, accent, style, and meaning

— thinking ahead for attacks and releases

— maintaining the even flow of a lyric melody

— accuracy of awkward intervals, chord changes, and modulatory passages

— awareness of like and unlike phrases—their musical and literary function within the song

— avoidance of common rhythmic errors such as

— attention to logical voice combinations when drilling parts

— attention to and awareness of other parts descending on a sustained part

— accuracy of humming parts

— attention to the problem of speed vs. volume

— practice of restraint and taste when executing expressive elements of the score

These aspects of good singing are easily demonstrated and experienced in artistic literature of good quality. Teenagers should sing and listen to many well-known art songs.

An excerpt from "Dedication" by Robert Franz appears on page 26. When singing this selection call attention to:

— the elements of tone quality that determine the expression

— the aspects of the text that are related to phrasing and dynamics

— the rise and fall of each phrase

— accurate releases on the rests

— subtlety of the dynamics

— accuracy of the ♩. ♫ pattern

— consonants and open vowels

— the intonation of the whole step interval (B—C-sharp) ascending followed by the half step interval descending (C—B) in measures 11, 12, and 14

Dedication

Wolfgang Müller
Translated by Francis Kingsley Ball

Robert Franz

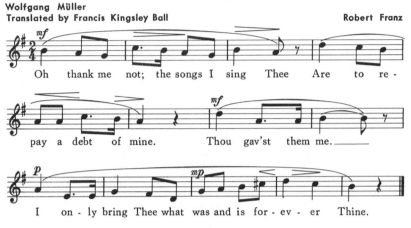

Oh thank me not; the songs I sing Thee Are to re -
pay a debt of mine. Thou gav'st them me.
I on - ly bring Thee what was and is for - ev - er Thine.

Copyright Ginn and Company. Used by permission.

Teaching Songs

SUGGESTED PROCEDURES FOR TEACHING ROTE SONGS

Effective procedures for teaching rote songs are invaluable to the junior high school music teacher.

 — 1. Motivate the students by creating a desire to learn the song.[2]
 — 2. Give students an opportunity to hear the entire song several times.
 — 3. If the song contains several verses with refrain, students may be able to join in the refrain after hearing the song a few times.
 — 4. Students listen while joining in the refrain.
 — 5. Sing the entire song. Isolate any difficult phrases.

REMEMBER Any specific procedure will depend upon the difficulty of the song, the ability of the group, and the ingenuity of the teacher. Maintain interest in rote singing by varying the modes of presentation and by limiting the amount of time spent on any one song.

SUGGESTED PROCEDURES FOR TEACHING PART SONGS WITH BOOKS

 — 1. Motivate the students by creating a desire to learn the song.
 — 2. Teacher plays the voice parts on the piano as each group follows its part in the book. A recorded arrangement could also be used.
 — 3. Students attempt to sing parts.
 — 4. Discuss such interesting characteristics of individual parts as entrances, repetitions, imitative passages, and intervals.

[2]Points of departure for motivation may be found on pp. 12–13.

— 5. Students in the lowest group sing their part.

— 6. Students in the next lowest group sing their part.

— 7. Combine the above two parts. (Continue until all parts have been combined.)

— 8. Students sing the entire song in parts.

— 9. When reviewing individual parts, make sure that students hear the entire harmonic context. This may be accomplished by having other parts hum or by playing all parts softly while emphasizing the part being reviewed.

Music Reading

Familiarity with the musical score and the ability to read music in a group establish a vocabulary which makes music more lasting and meaningful. Teaching practices involved in the development of comprehensive reading should be based upon aural concepts derived from a musical context rather than those which are contrived. In the junior high school music class, it would seem that the reading of music should be incorporated into the performance and study of the music itself.[3] The following are points of departure for lessons involving music reading:

— isolation and reading of melodic and rhythmic passages in songs

— performing interesting rhythm patterns from notation

— notation of accompaniments played on various classroom instruments

— notation of original songs and melodic fragments

— notation of chords as they are sung and played

— observation of notated themes and utilization of scores while listening

— comparison of like and unlike tonal and rhythmic patterns as found in like and unlike phrases

REMEMBER   Those students requiring a *high* level of individual music reading proficiency are usually those most likely to be studying music privately.

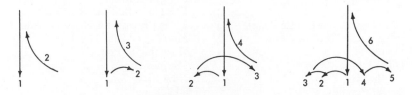

Conducting patterns.

[3]Because music reading should not be an isolated activity, it has been incorporated into lessons on the elements of music. See these sections for suggestions.

Assembly and Recreational Singing

In junior high school, music is often a part of assembly programs. The following are general suggestions for planning an assembly sing.

— may be planned by the music class

— may utilize unison and harmony songs learned in class

— may include rhythmic accompaniments with some appropriate songs

— may include a variety of material—rounds and canons; fun and action songs; songs of varying moods; suitable current songs; and so forth

— may incorporate descants by special groups

— may include the learning of new songs

— may feature a special attraction by a solo or small group of students or faculty

The range for unison singing is:

REMEMBER   A *well-played* accompaniment always enhances the singing experience.

SUGGESTED SONGS

For assembly and recreational purposes, students enjoy singing patriotic songs, spirituals, folk songs, show tunes, seasonal, and nonsense songs. The following list represents a random selection of favorites.

All Night, All Day
America
America the Beautiful
Anchors Aweigh
Army Goes Rolling Along
Battle Hymn of the Republic
Bells of St. Mary's, The
Bicycle Built for Two
Camptown Races
Capital Ship
Chiapenecas
Chumbara
Dear Hearts and Gentle People
Deep in the Heart of Texas
Do Lord
Don't Fence Me In
Do-Re-Mi
Easter Parade
Ev'ry Time I Feel the Spirit
God Bless America

Go Down Moses
Green Grow the Rushes, O
Happy Wanderer, The
He's Got the Whole World in His Hands
Home on the Range
It's a Small, Small World
I've Got Sixpence
I Whistle a Happy Tune
Jacob's Ladder
Kum Ba Yah
Let There Be Peace on Earth
Little Brown Church in the Vale
Marching Along Together
Marching to Pretoria
Marines Hymn
New River Train
Oklahoma!
Oh, What a Beautiful Morning
Red, Red Robin

Sailing, Sailing
Sit Down Sister
She'll Be Comin' Round the
   Mountain
Star Spangled Banner
Swanee River
Swing Low, Sweet Chariot
Tell Me Why
This Is My Country

This Land Is Your Land
When the Saints Go Marching In
You're a Grand Old Flag
Wagon Wheels
Waltzing Matilda
While Strolling Through the Park
Zulu Warrior
Yellow Bird

3

Music Listening

Teacher: *"What kind of music do you like to listen to?"*

Student: *"I don't know because I don't listen very often."*

The primary goal of the listening program in the junior high school is the enjoyment derived from listening to music of lasting value. Music of good quality should have a natural appeal to students provided they actually listen to what is contained in the music they hear. In other words, a mere auditory reaction to the physical sound is not the only factor in a *comprehensive* perception of music. The sound heard physically must be attended to before actual listening takes place.

If students are to derive lasting values from the listening program in school, they should receive guidance in detecting the elements common to most music, i.e., melody, rhythm, harmony, and tone color form. Such guidance should allow the student to discover and actively listen to the communicative aspects of worth-while compositions. As a result, they will respond to unfamiliar music with interest and will continue to listen in later life.

The following are examples of lines of questioning to aid student discovery.

— What is it in the sound that _____ ?
— Which musical elements lead you to think that _____ ?
— Are there any musical clues as to the country from which this music might come?
— Is your ear more quickly attracted to the melody, rhythm, or harmony of this composition?
— If you were going to compose a piece of program music to describe a _____ , what might it sound like?
— How did the composer use music to describe _____ ?

— If you were the composer or arranger, how would you put _____ melody into an orchestral setting?

— Would raising or lowering the pitch change the mood of the composition? How?

— Of what value is repetition in this music?

— How would removing or replacing the bar lines affect this work?

— What must the composer consider before choosing a particular tone color?

Students listen while following the score.

REMEMBER "Listening can only be really alive when there are listeners who are really alive. To listen intently, to listen consciously, to listen with one's whole intelligence is the least we can do in the furtherance of an art that is one of the glories of mankind."

Aaron Copland

Listening While Singing And Playing Instruments

1. Write the rhythm pattern on page 32 on the board above a staff.
2. Class attempts to identify this familiar tune by attention to rhythm pattern. ("Are You Sleeping?")[1]

[1] As a followup, students may enjoy listening to the Third Movement, *First Symphony*, Gustav Mahler which includes this melody in altered form.

3. Class claps (or taps) rhythm to check the accuracy of identification.

4. Teacher indicates the number (or syllable) of the starting tone. (C)

5. Class studies the first phrase *silently*, attempting to hear the number names of the tones.

6. Class sings the first phrase aloud with number names as the teacher writes appropriate number above each note.

7. Repeat this procedure with each phrase.

8. Class sings the entire song with numbers.

9. Student(s) notates the melody on a staff below the rhythmic notation. (C major)

10. Add bells and/or piano as the class sings from the notation on board.

11. Class studies the possible chord outlined by the melody and discovers the chord for each phrase.

12. Student writes the letter chord symbols on board.

13. Play the chords on autoharp and/or piano as the class sings.

14. Discuss transposition.

15. Class indicates the letter chord symbols in at least three other keys.

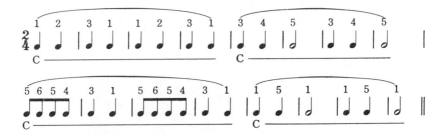

Try other melodies using this procedure:

Merrily We Roll Along
Hot Cross Buns
Row, Row, Row Your Boat
Brahms' "Lullaby"
Battle Hymn of the Republic (chorus)
Theme from Andante Movement of Haydn's "Surprise" Symphony (first 4 measures)

Listening to Harmonize

1. Place words (only) for the song on page 33 on the board.

2. Sing the song.[2] Discover the meter and mark off measures.

3. Discover like and unlike melodic phrases.

4. Divide the class into two groups—one sings the melody as the other sings "one" on G.

[2]For variations on "Ach du lieber Augustin" see page 93.

5. Students discover inappropriate measures for the "one" (1) chord harmony.

6. Play (or sing) the root of the V chord for the class.

7. Students select measures (by ear) for substitutions of the V chord.

8. Write the roots of I, V, I on the board as the students sing.

9. Repeat the entire song with one group singing the melody and the other singing "one" and "five" as the harmony changes.

10. Try other melodies: "Home on the Range" (I, IV, V); "Sweet Betsy from Pike" (I, IV, V); "Stodala Pumpa" (I, V); "Streets of Laredo" (I, V).

The More We Get Together
(Ach du lieber Augustin)

REMEMBER The purpose of these lessons is primarily *aural.* The integration of visual symbols *derived* from the sound is an excellent reinforcement for the ear.

Listening Lessons

In the following listening lessons, notate the suggested themes on the board or overhead projector transparency. As the music is being heard, present the questions for student discovery. Depending upon the approach, the notated themes may be presented before, during, or after the music is heard.

34

SEMPER FIDELIS MARCH (B SECTION), Sousa

FROM NOTATION

1. Play, sing, and tap the rhythm of each melody.

2. Discover the structural characteristics of each melody (chord, scale, rhythm, etc.).

3. Before listening to the recording, class suggests the order of melodic entrance and the instruments they might use if they were the composer.

4. While listening, discover the entrance of each melody and follow from visual notation.

Symphony No.1 in C Major,

THIRD MOVEMENT

Beethoven

QUESTIONS FOR STUDENT DISCOVERY

1. What musical term describes the opening theme of the Minuet? (G major scale)

2. Is this the particular scale you would expect by looking at the key signature? (no) Why? (key signature implies C major or A minor) What can you find in the score that prevents this theme from being C major? (F sharp)

3. After listening to the entire movement, how many times and with what changes does Beethoven repeat this theme? (six times)

4. Clap or tap the rhythm of this theme. Play it on the piano in rhythm. Make up a different rhythm. For example:

5. What chord does Beethoven use in the beginning of the Trio? (C major) Listen to the harmony shift to a new chord. (A minor) Play these two chords on the piano.

6. As a follow-up, listen to the opening measures of the fourth movement of the same symphony. In what ways is it the same as the third? In what ways is it different?

FOURTH MOVEMENT

IN THE STEPPES OF CENTRAL ASIA,[3] Alexander Borodin

Acquaint the students with the following description of *In the Steppes of Central Asia* which Borodin placed on the orchestral score: "In the silence of the monotonous steppes of Central Asia is heard the sound of peaceful Russian song. From the distance we hear the approach of horses and camels and the bizarre and melancholy notes of an oriental melody. A caravan approaches, escorted by Russian soldiers and continues safely on its way through the immense desert. The notes of the Russian and Asiatic melodies join in common harmony, which dies away as the caravan disappears in the distance."

Before listening to the music, discuss the following questions:

How might music for this description sound?
What types of melodies would be appropriate?
Which orchestral instruments will probably be featured?

THEME 1

Allegretto con moto

p cantabile

dim.

THEME 2

Cantabile ed expressivo

p

COMBINED THEMES

cantabile

---

[3]*Adventures in Music*, VI, Vol. 1, R.C.A. See *Teacher's Guide* for more background information on the composer, highlights of the music, and additional suggestions. Theme Two is also found in the Broadway musical *Kismet*.

QUESTIONS FOR STUDENT DISCOVERY

1. In what way was each of the two themes appropriate to the description?

2. Using only these two themes, how did Borodin achieve variety in this composition?

3. Why were the two themes played simultaneously? Looking at the notation, how is theme two changed when joined with theme one?

4. Can you place on the board musical symbols which describe the dynamics?

5. Why do you think Borodin used these markings?

6. Which orchestral instruments introduced each theme? Relate to the description.

7. How is the tone produced on the low string instruments as they play the following rhythmic accompaniment?

HUNGARIAN RHAPSODY NO. 1, Liszt

Students are usually very interested in the many imaginative ways a composer uses the orchestra to elaborate simple and familiar melodies. Liszt used the Hungarian song "Where the Cranes Fly" in his first *Hungarian Rhapsody*. Students should be familiar with the song before the orchestral work is introduced.

Where the Cranes Fly

Hungarian Song

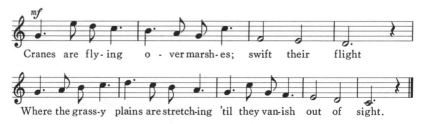

Cranes are fly-ing o-ver marsh-es; swift their flight

Where the grass-y plains are stretch-ing 'til they van-ish out of sight.

Copyright Ginn and Company. Used by permission.

QUESTIONS FOR STUDENT DISCOVERY

1. What does the word "rhapsody" mean?

2. Listen to the introduction. In which register is the "Crane" theme first heard? (low)

3. Listen to the entire *Rhapsody*. What unifies the composition? ("Crane" theme) Does the "Crane" theme sound the same each time it is heard? Replay each alteration of the "Crane" theme. How is it different each time? (instrumentation, syncopated, changing register, dynamics)

4. Listen again. In what other ways is variety achieved? (variation of the "Crane" theme, introduction of contrasting themes)

5. Discuss the tone color and use of dynamics in the rhapsody form.

A LINCOLN PORTRAIT,[4] Aaron Copland

Tell students that they are going to hear a composition by one of America's greatest composers, AARON COPLAND, 1900– . He wrote this music to describe one of America's greatest presidents. Ask students if they were composers, which president they would choose to describe. Copland chose Lincoln and entitled the work, "A Lincoln Portrait." Discuss the meaning of the word "portrait"; ask if a portrait describes only *physical* appearance.

Have students list characteristics of Lincoln, as the teacher writes them on the board in three basic categories:

Ex. strong	quiet	sense of humor
tall	gentle	
courageous	sensitive	
patriotic		
disturbed		

[4]This music is included in #75, *U.S. History in Music*, Bowmar Orchestral Library. Another excellent recording is Columbia MS6684 (Philadelphia Orchestra).

(Prepared by Susan Peterson, Music Education Staff, University of Colorado.)

THEME 1

THEME 2

On Spring-field Moun - tain   Once did   dwell   A   hand-some youth,

I   knew him   well

THEME 3

Allegro moderato

1. Display or project three theme charts.

2. Listen to the first part of Theme 1 on recording. Students identify with corresponding theme chart and relate to proper list of adjectives. Discuss how Theme 1 describes these characteristics (strong, courageous, etc.).
   —strong, dotted rhythmic effect
   —slow, steady tempo
   —use of open fourths and fifths
   —repetition
   —register ranging from very high to very low
   —fortissimo
   —strings and brass

3. Play first part of Theme 2 on recording. Is Theme 2 familiar? (Copland borrowed Theme 2 from a folk song that was popular

in Lincoln's day called "On Springfield Mountain" which may be sung later). Discuss how Theme 2 describes Lincoln (quiet, gentle, sensitive).

—simple melody and harmony

—slow, steady tempo

—legato

—pianissimo

—woodwinds

4. Play first part of Theme 3 on recording. Is Theme 3 familiar? Copland borrowed Stephen Foster's "Camptown Races," although he altered it slightly (may be sung later). Discuss how Theme 3 describes Lincoln's sense of humor.

—catchy melody and rhythm

—lively, steady tempo

—staccato

—strings

5. Listen to the entire recording. Over a period of time, focus attention on:

—why the composition sounds so American

—following entrances of the three themes

—changes in tempo

—changes in dynamics

—changes in instrumentation

—variation of themes

—use of more than one theme at a time

—use of themes as background for narration

Two Related Listening Lessons

In the literature of music there are many compositions which may be paired for the purpose of musical comparison. Two programmatic pieces which fall into this category are "Troika" from *Lieutenant Kije Suite* by Prokofiev, and "Sleigh Ride" by LeRoy Anderson.

QUESTIONS FOR STUDENT DISCOVERY

1. Listen to "Troika." Does the music describe the meaning of the word "troika"?

2. Which musical elements contribute to the description of a sleigh ride?

3. If you were composing a piece of program music to describe a sleigh ride, how would it sound?

4. Listen to "Sleigh Ride." How are the compositions alike? How are they different? Which composer uses more sound effects?

5. Sing "Troika." (*Music for Everyone*, Prentice-Hall, Inc.) Add sleigh bell accompaniment.

6. If you were to receive one of these recordings as a Christmas present, which would you prefer? Why?

REMEMBER   Theoretical analysis need not be a part of every listening experience in the music class.

4

Playing Instruments

Playing instruments is an excellent way to develop sensitivity to both the theoretical and expressive aspects of music such as melodic, rhythmic, and harmonic structure; phrasing; dynamics; and tone-color.

Essential to the success of most instrumental work in the general music classroom is planning and organization. Even experienced teachers note the importance of efficient methods for tuning, distribution, and collection of instruments in addition to a well designed instructional plan.

Planning should not, of course, hamper the student in terms of his creative expression. In fact, there are many types of lessons in which the student will experience considerable freedom in the exploration of sound media, creative composition, and use of synthetic sounds, etc.

Suggested Instruments

Melodic	*Rhythmic*	*Harmonic*
Keyboard	Keyboard	Keyboard
Resonator Bells	Drums	Autoharp
Psaltery	Maracas	Harmolin
Recorder	Finger Cymbals	Ukulele
Song Flute	Triangle	Guitar
Orchestral Instruments	Gong	Bass Viol
	Claves	
	Castanets	
	Woodblock	

Media for Playing Instruments

RHYTHM CHANTS AND ROUNDS

There are many musical and literary forms that lend themselves to classroom experiences with musical instruments. The following is an example stressing dynamics. Select instruments by experimentation.

Bang, Bong, Noisy Beat!

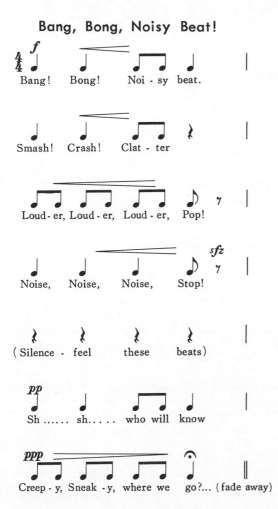

Bang! Bong! Noi - sy beat.

Smash! Crash! Clat - ter

Loud - er, Loud - er, Loud - er, Pop!

Noise, Noise, Noise, Stop!

(Silence - feel these beats)

Sh ...... sh..... who will know

Creep - y, Sneak - y, where we go?... (fade away)

From *Rhythm in Music and Dance for Children* by Sally Monsour, Marilyn Chambers Cohen, and Patricia Eckert Lindell. © 1966 by Wadsworth Publishing Company, Inc., Belmont, California. Reprinted by permission of the publisher.

The Weather Man

Zoe Ann Kelley

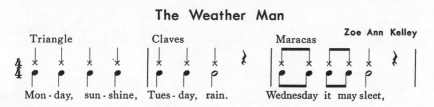

Triangle   Claves   Maracas

Mon - day, sun - shine, Tues - day, rain.   Wednesday it may sleet,

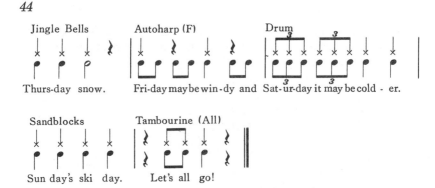

In "Instrumental Addition" each instrument starts as it is mentioned in the chant. It may also be played in accumulative fashion—each instrument continuing with its own rhythm pattern after it has entered. Several days later, the student may notate the rhythm of the particular instrument he wishes to play.

Instrumental Addition

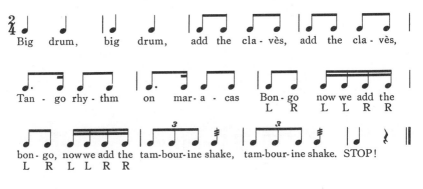

JAM SESSION

Students enjoy improvising rhythm patterns. One student begins with a basic drum beat, such as: ♩ ♩ ♩ ♩ | etc. Other rhythm instruments join in, one at a time, adding their own patterns.

WHO'S WHO?

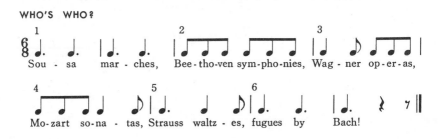

SONGS

Songs provide an excellent opportunity for playing a variety of musical accompaniments. It is usually desirable to add instrumental parts after the students have learned the song.

Long John

Copyright Beatrice Landeck. Courtesy of David McKay Co., Inc.

Add a piano accompaniment:

F   Gm   Am   Gm   etc.

1. Write chord names under staff.
2. Students play chords on keyboard replicas as one student plays piano. (See Half Step Formula, page 74.)
3. Students notate chords on staff.
4. Student(s) plays chord accompaniment as class sings "Long John."
5. Add afterbeat rhythm:

clap

snap

etc.

Good Night Ladies

Tune Ukulele

Ukulele

F   C⁷

Goodnight ladies, goodnight ladies,

F   B♭   F   C⁷   F

Goodnight ladies, we're going to leave you now.

F   C⁷   F

Merrily we roll along, roll along, roll along,

F   C⁷   F

Merrily we roll along, o'er the deep blue sea.

[5]These chords may also be played on the top four strings of the guitar. More chording suggestions with guitar and uke are found in current music books for students.

5

Understanding Melody

"The melody is generally what the piece is about." (Aaron Copland)

The understanding and enjoyment of melody comes from repeated experiences with specific melodies of many types. If students are expected to gain a means for continued appreciation of melodies in later life, they should become acquainted with melodies of varying shapes and tonal centers.

Characteristics

— direction—upward, downward
— range—wide, narrow
— register—low, middle, high
— length—short, long
— structure—stepwise, skipwise, scalewise, chordwise
— rhythm—patterns
— mode—major, minor, pentatonic
— other—color, dynamics, phrasing, climax, etc.

Study the characteristics of melody in familiar and unfamiliar settings. Compare one type of melody with another. Discuss the manner in which the characteristics combine to create interesting and beautiful melodies.

EXAMPLES
ONCE TO EVERY MAN AND NATION
(stepwise; rhythm)

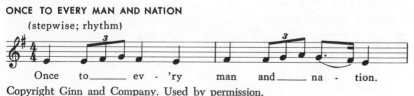

Once to_____ ev - 'ry   man   and_____ na - tion.

Copyright Ginn and Company. Used by permission.

CLASSICAL SYMPHONY, THIRD MOVEMENT, Prokofiev

(stepwise; skipwise; octave; wide range)

Copyright 1926 by Edition Russe de Musique. Reprinted by permission of Boosey & Hawkes, Inc., Assignees of the Copyright.

WALTZ FROM ROSENKAVALIER SUITE, Strauss

(skipwise; wide range; long; rhythm)

Copyright 1911 by A. Furstner, Renewed 1938. Copyright and Renewal assigned to Boosey & Hawkes Inc. Reprinted by permission.

ALPINE SYMPHONY ("NIGHT" THEME), Strauss

(long; downward; scalewise; rhythm register)

Lento

Copyright FEC Leuckart. Courtesy of Associated Music Publishers, Inc.

"BARCAROLE" FROM TALES OF HOFFMAN, Offenbach

(stepwise; rhythm; narrow range)

MY HEART EVER FAITHFUL, Bach

(rhythm; stepwise; skipwise)

"BUCKAROO HOLIDAY" FROM RODEO, Copland
(downward; scalewise)

Copyright 1946 by Hawkes & Son (London) Ltd. Reprinted by permission.

THE STAR - SPANGLED BANNER
(chordwise)

O   say   can   you   see.

SABRE DANCE, Khachaturian
(repeated; narrow range)
Marcatissimo

Sabre Dance from *Gayne* by Aram Khachaturian. © Copyright 1948 by MCA Music, a division of MCA Inc., New York, New York. Used by permission. All rights reserved.

REMEMBER We are attracted to many beautiful melodies because of their expressive and elusive qualities. Incorporate phrasing, dynamics, climax, tempo, and tone color into lessons on melody. Descriptive phrases and illustrative designs may also reinforce the "feeling" which melodies produce.

Teaching Suggestions

Although melody cannot be separated from the other elements of music, there are many compositions in which the melody stands out. When teaching melodic structure, these should be utilized as frequently as possible.

Approach the study of melody through singing and playing instruments as well as listening. Formulate questions regarding melodic structure and help students to discover the answers. The following list may suggest points of departure for such questions. It is also important to repeat melodic concepts often and to transfer these concepts to new compositions.

QUESTIONS ABOUT MELODY

— What is the general shape of the melody?

— Is the melody angular or circular in feeling?

— Does the melody move in scale or chord progression?

— Is the melody lyric, easy to sing? How many phrases does it have?

— Are the phrases long, short, easy to hear and locate?

— Is the range of the melody wide or narrow?

— In which vocal range can the melody be found?

— What is the relationship between the range of the melody and the instrument for which it is written?

— Is the melody stated in *your* vocal range?

— How many different melodies can be heard in the composition?

— What distinguishes one melody from another?

— Does the period or style in which the melody was composed have anything to do with its range, shape, or structure?

— Would the melody be satisfying without the harmony?

— Are there any fragments of the melody in the harmony or in the accompaniment?

— Could the melody be transposed to another key or mode and remain appropriate to its text or musical setting?

— Does the tempo of the melody convey the general mood?

— Could the tempo be changed? How? Why?

— Is the melody strongly accented? Why?

— Could the melody be altered, added to? How?

— Are there any sequences or imitative passages in the melody? Where?

REMEMBER Melodies become meaningful when their underlying unity is perceived. For this reason students should *not* be taught to listen to melody as a series of single tones, but to a melodic line as a whole.

Melodic Variations

The possibilities for varying one melody are practically unlimited. The following variations by Mozart indicate what can happen to a simple melody when it is "dressed up." Discover the manner in which the elements of music are changed in each variation.

Variations on "Twinkle, Twinkle" Little Star

Mozart

How   I   won - der   what   you ____ are.

Var. I
Moderato

Var. II
Allegro

Var. III
Andante

Var. IV
Allegro

Melodic Style

Melodic style is directly related to the historical period in which the music was written. Individual composers also possess their own unique musical style. As an example, F. Wayne Scott has written a series of variations on "Hot Cross Buns," each of which depicts a different dance style.

Students sing "Hot Cross Buns" as teacher plays each stylistic variation on the piano. Appropriate instruments should be added as an aid in interpretation.

Variations on "Hot Cross Buns"

Dances New   F. Wayne Scott
Waltz: ♩ = 144

Square Dance: Lively

Used by permission.

Tango: ♩ = 72

Blues: ♩ = 66

Dances Old
Minuet: ♩ = 120

Sarabande: ♩ = 96

Gavotte: ♩ = 60

Gigue: ♩ = 120

Classroom Study of Twelve-tone Row

Before experimenting with the twelve-tone row, students should listen to and discuss the sound of music which includes this compositional technique. For example: *Suite for Piano*, Schoenberg; Opening section, Third Movement. *Fourth String Quartet*, Schoenberg.[2] Students will also enjoy hearing twelve-tone music played by their classmates.[3]

Introductory Activity[4]

1. Select 12 students to stand facing the class in a single line. Count off from 1 to 12 beginning at the left.
2. Arrange twelve individual resonator bells in chromatic position beginning with C.
3. Each student then selects any resonator bell of his choice at random, returning to his place in the row.
4. Listen as each person sounds his resonator bell beginning at the left.
5. The twelve sounds become a twelve-tone row. Each student plays his bell in turn, beginning from the right of the row. This results in what is termed "retrograde."

It should be established that no tone may be sounded twice in succession; nor can a tone be repeated until each of the other eleven tones has been used.

Follow-up by composing four measures of music using the tone row derived in the above activity. The following is a suggested procedure.

1. Decide on a meter and a rather slow tempo.
2. Divide the twelve students into four committees with each committee responsible for planning the pattern of rhythm for one measure:

   Measure I, students 1 and 2
   Measure II, students 3, 4, and 5
   Measure III, students 6, 7, 8, 9, and 10
   Measure IV, students 11 and 12
3. Establish the tempo by counting aloud.

[2]"Peripetia" from *Five Pieces for Orchestra*, Schoenberg (Bowmar Orchestral Library #86). (See Appendix F for a list of Recordings of Contemporary Music.)
[3]Examples are the pieces of Ross Lee Finney, found in the Frances Clarke Library, *Contemporary Piano Literature*, Book 4 and 6, Summy-Birchard Publishing Co., 1961. Also, suggestions on twentieth-century composition may be found in *Exploring Music, Junior Book*, Holt, Rinehart, and Winston, Inc., 1968.
[4]Parts of this procedure were taken from the *Arizona Guide for Teaching Music in the Elementary Schools*, 1966.

4. Ask each committee to perform in turn. Notate.

5. Perform the composition from notation. Add percussion instruments with contrasting rhythm patterns.

The following example was composed by a group of seventh graders using the procedures above. Notice that the students composed the last four measures with the tone row in retrograde using different rhythm.

Lessons in Miniature

1. *Toccata in G Major, Bach*

— Contrast the two distinct types of melodic structure.

— Discuss the downward tendency of the direction.

— Notice the solid descending chords that seem to summarize the two basic musical ideas.

2. Theme from "Jupiter," *The Planets* and the anthem, "I Vow to Thee My Country," Holst.

I Vow to Thee, My Country

Sir Cecil Spring-Rice

Gustav Holst

I vow to thee, my coun - try, all earth - ly things a -
And there's an - oth - er coun - try, I've heard of long a -

bove, En - tire and whole and per - fect, the ser-vice of my
go, Most dear to them that love her, most great to them that

love; The love that asks no question, the love that stands the
know; We my not count her ar - mies, we may not see her

test, That lays up-on the al - tar the dear-est and the best;
King; Her for-tress is a faith-ful heart her pride is suf - fering

The love that ne - ver fal - ters, the love that pays the price,
And soul by soul and si-lent-ly, her shin-ing bounds in - crease,

The love that makes un-daunted the fi - nal sac - ri - fice.
And her ways are ways of gentle - ness and all her paths are peace.

Copyright J. Curwen and Sons, Ltd., used by permission. Single harmonized copies may be obtained from J. Curwen, 29 Maiden Lane, London, England (one shilling).

— Notice the broad sweeping flow of this melody.
— Discuss the relationship of the text and the melody.
— Sing the melody expressing the mood of the text.
— Relate this anthem to the middle section of "Jupiter" by G. Holst, the theme from which it was taken.

3. "America."

etc.

— Play "America" shifting register for each tone.
— Discuss the disjointed effect of these shifts.
— Experiment with shifting registers (octave displacement) using other familiar melodies.

4. *Introduction to Concerto for Orchestra,* Bartok

Copyright 1946 by Hawkes & Son (London) Ltd. Reprinted by permission.

— Notice the rise and fall of the pitch line.
— Discover the use of the fourth as a basic interval.
— Discuss the structure of melodies based on various intervals such as thirds, sixths, etc.

5. Melodies and Recorded Themes[5] Based on a tonic triad.

STAR-SPANGLED BANNER

BUGLE CALL

[5]A suggested reference for lessons involving thematic structure is *Dictionary of Musical Themes*, Harold Barlow and Sam Morgenstern, Crown Pub., 1948.

MARINES' HYMN

PRELUDE #1. WELL-TEMPERED CLAVIER, Bach

SYMPHONY NO. 6, FIFTH MOVEMENT
(FIRST THEME), Beethoven

RUMANIAN RHAPSODY NO. 1
(FIRST THEME), Enesco

— Identify the song titles from notation.

— Compare via direction, even or uneven rhythm, and so forth.

— Relate the discussion of structural concepts to the recorded examples.

6

Understanding Rhythm

Rhythm is an essential ingredient in music and should, therefore, assume a central place within the content of the junior high school music class. Many musical compositions are more quickly identified and enjoyed because of the rhythmic element. In addition, all music will be better appreciated when the listener or performer is aware of the expressive elements inherent in the rhythm. Most students are attracted to the rhythmic structure of compositions and will respond with enthusiasm to lessons which are planned around this element.

Characteristics

— underlying pulse
— meter
— accent
— syncopation, afterbeat
— typical patterns
— other—tempo, rubato, dynamics, color, ritard, accelerando, etc.

Media for Rhythm Study

SONGS

— Clap the rhythm and underlying beat of many songs.
— Compose original counter-rhythms and notate.
— Use rhythm instruments to accompany songs.
— Discuss and utilize symbols and words which express rhythm, meter and tempo.

RECORDINGS

— Listen for the characteristic rhythm of compositions.
— Listen for rhythmic contrasts.
— Listen and discuss the identifiable rhythm of various dance forms.

SYMPHONY NO. 7, SECOND MOVEMENT, Beethoven

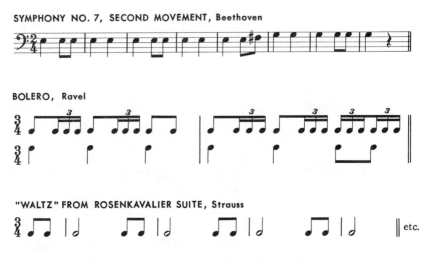

BOLERO, Ravel

"WALTZ" FROM ROSENKAVALIER SUITE, Strauss

DANCES: FOLK, TRADITIONAL, CREATIVE

If words are sung, teach song first followed by actions. Express phrasing, design of the music, or rhythmic structure through body movement. (The nature of this activity should be suited to the interest level of junior high school students.)

RHYTHMIC CHANTS AND ROUNDS

— Chant rhythm rounds. Execute both aurally and with notation. Add instruments.

— Devise visual drills containing elements of musical interest.

— Make sure the rhythm is felt as well as understood metrically.

— Use instruments.

— Chant and notate words, poems or literary works containing a variety of rhythmic patterns. Use instruments to emphasize quality, accent, and so forth. The following are some examples.

Football

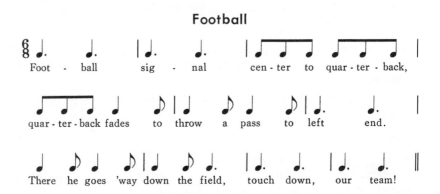

Foot - ball sig - nal cen - ter to quar - ter - back,

quar - ter - back fades to throw a pass to left end.

There he goes 'way down the field, touch down, our team!

National Parks

Judith Dodge Breneman

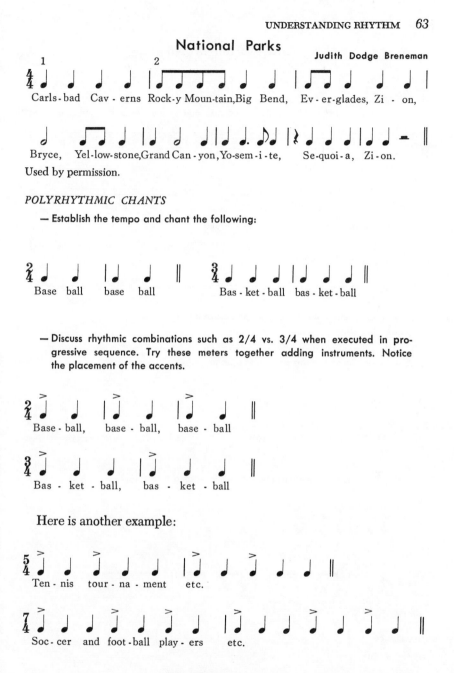

Carls-bad Cav - erns Rock-y Moun-tain, Big Bend, Ev - er-glades, Zi - on,

Bryce, Yel-low-stone, Grand Can - yon, Yo-sem - i - te, Se-quoi - a, Zi - on.

Used by permission.

POLYRHYTHMIC CHANTS

— Establish the tempo and chant the following:

Base ball base ball

Bas - ket - ball bas - ket - ball

— Discuss rhythmic combinations such as 2/4 vs. 3/4 when executed in pro-
gressive sequence. Try these meters together adding instruments. Notice
the placement of the accents.

Base - ball, base - ball, base - ball

Bas - ket - ball, bas - ket - ball

Here is another example:

Ten - nis tour - na - ment etc.

Soc - cer and foot - ball play - ers etc.

Teaching Lessons

As with melody, rhythm study should be derived from interesting
musical material. The following lesson involves a study of time values.

Old Abram Brown

English

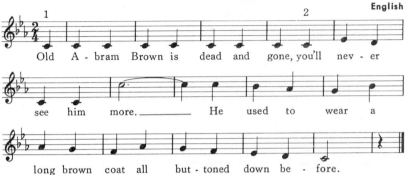

Old A - bram Brown is dead and gone, you'll nev - er

see him more._____ He used to wear a

long brown coat all but - toned down be - fore.

Copyright 1936 by Boosey & Company Ltd. Reprinted by permission. (Choral arrangements are also available.)

1. Sing "Old Abram Brown" in rather strict time accenting the primary beat slightly.
2. Sing as a round—basses double an octave lower.
3. Add low drum in steady quarter notes.
4. A few alto-tenors may sing the following part *listening* for the dissonance as it occurs. Reinforce this part on the piano.

Old A - bram Brown is dead and gone, you'll

5. Try the following rhythmic changes while singing as a round.

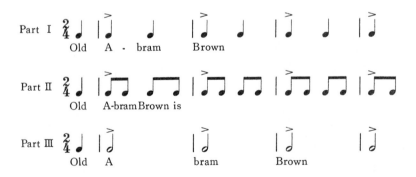

6. Each part begins his own rhythm upon entrance. When the third part has entered, three different patterns will be sung simultaneously.
7. To develop further sensitivity to dissonance, the teacher may select a particular spot within the composition and, upon cue, the students should hold their respective tones and listen.

ACCENT

Repeat the words "East Pole" in rapid succession. Soon you will find yourself saying "Police." The meaning of whole sentences can sometimes be changed by the manner in which we emphasize, accent or punctuate. The same can be said of musical symbols and meanings.

THE LAST FIVE MINUTES

Shown above is an excerpt from "The Last Five Minutes."[1] It exemplifies the importance of accent in a musical composition.

Play the first five tones of the scale several times without accent before adding the accompaniment. The result will be obvious!

SHIFTING ACCENTS

Listen to the excerpt from the *Hary Janos Suite* by Kodaly. Attention should be called to the shifting accents created by the meter of the five notes in the piano part.

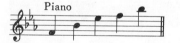

"VIENNESE MUSICAL CLOCK" FROM HARY JANOS SUITE, Kodaly

Copyright 1927 by Universal Edition, Renewed 1955. Sole Agents for U.S.A. and Canada, Boosey & Hawkes Inc. Reprinted by permission.

[1] J. Clovis and E. Nelson, "The Last Five Minutes" (New York: Mills Music, Inc., 1952).

66

ACCENT VS. DURATION

The two patterns below contain identical time values in terms of duration but they are quite different when actually sounded. Try clapping each separately, then together. Use two different rhythm instruments to vary the quality of sound. This will bring out the shift in accent.

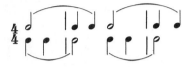

RHYTHMIC INTENSITY

Intensity in music need not always be obtained by an increase in dynamics. The following is an example of increased intensity by means of rhythm.

Shalom Chaverim

Israeli Round

Sha - lom* cha-ver-im,† sha- lom cha-ver-im, Sha - lom, sha - lom. Le -

hit - ra - ot,†† le - hit - ra - ot, Sha - lom, sha - lom.

Cooperative Recreation Service. Used by permission.

1. Add the following rhythmic patterns in sequence:

2. Add the following melodic chant:

sha - lom_____   sha - lom_____

SYNCOPATION

1. Learn "Canoe Song." Add alto-tenor descant with the melody and words of "dip, dip, and swing."

2. Add instruments to reinforce the rhythm. Notice the syncopation.

Canoe Song

My pad - dle's keen and bright, Flash - ing   with sil - ver.

Fol - low   the wild goose flight,   Dip, dip   and swing.

From *Adventures in Song*, 1940, Cooperative Recreation Service. Used by permission.

3. Sing "Canoe Song" without syncopation:

My   pad-dle's keen and bright,

4. Discover the effect caused by the absence of syncopation.

MORE SYNCOPATION[2]

1. Sing "Rock Island Line."

2. Add the final consonant of "Rock" to the first vowel of "Island" in order to emphasize the syncopation.

[2]"Symphonic Dances" from *West Side Story*, Leonard Bernstein, are excellent examples of various kinds of rhythmic structure. (This recording is included in *Discovering Music Together*, Book viii, Follett.)

68

Rock Island Line

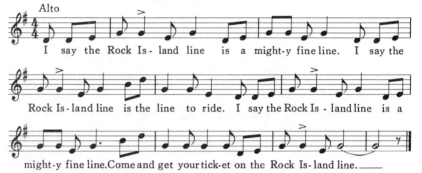

I say the Rock Is-land line is a might-y fine line. I say the

Rock Is-land line is the line to ride. I say the Rock Is-land line is a

might-y fine line. Come and get your tick-et on the Rock Is-land line. ____

From MUSIC IN OUR LIFE, © 1959, Silver Burdette Company.

For variety:

    3. Combine alto melody and soprano descant.

Rock Is-land line ____

    4. Combine basses on melody with alto-tenor descant.

Rock Is-land line ____

    5. Combine basses and altos on melody with soprano and alto-tenor descants.
    6. Combine alto melody with two descants and bass chant.

choo choo choo choo

Lessons in Miniature

1. "America, the Beautiful"

Rhythmic variations by Robert B. Glasgow. Used by permission.

- Chant words and clap each new rhythmic variation.
- Discuss each variation in terms of even or uneven pattern, change of meter, and text alignment.
- Create additional variations. Try alternating meters.

2. "Yankee Doodle"

- After clapping the rhythm of the original song, try altered version and notate "by ear."
- Discuss other examples of altered meter. Experiment with other familiar songs.

3. "Opening theme" from *Rite of Spring*, Stravinsky

— Listen for the frequent changes of meter.

— Discuss the mood this technique establishes for this particular piece of music.

4. "Andalucian Ballad," Arab Folk Tradition originating in Spain (twelfth century)

Not too fast

Melody instruments and voice on "Loo"

DRUM:

PIANO: Play melody in octaves with improvised embellishments.

From *Songs from the Arab World of the Near East* by Sally Monsour, Bowmar Records, Inc., 1969. Used by permission.

— Improvise other drum accompaniments in 9/4 meter in addition to that given above.

— Create a text to fit with this style and meter.

5. "Three to Get Ready," Dave Brubeck (Recording: *Time Out*, CL-1397).

— Discover the alternation of two measures each in 3/4 and 4/4 meter.

— Divide the class for alternate clapping (clap, snap, snap).

— Another time, add instruments or conduct in alternate groups.

6. "Blue Rondo a la Turk," Dave Brubeck (Recording: *Time Out*, CL-1397).

— After listening to the recording, notice the musical effect created by alternating three measures of the first accented grouping with one measure of the second.

— Discuss the variation of accent and its importance in music.

7

Understanding Harmony

Students in junior high school should become acquainted with two distinct types of harmonic structure—homophonic and polyphonic. Sing, play, and listen to a variety of compositions which exemplify both of these types.

Homophonic—one main melody, harmony supporting.

Polyphonic—two or more melodies sounding simultaneously.

Building Basic Chords

The following is a suggested procedure for developing perception of harmony which is essentially homophonic. Many of the steps will seem obvious to some teachers. However, there will be situations in which students have had little background in chord structures, indicating a need for basic explanations and procedures. This procedure is not intended as a lesson plan for one day. It may take several weeks.

1. **Sing a chord.**

    Hello   Hello   Hello   Hello

    (Basses may sing a low C on the fourth entrance.)

2. Sing the above chord beginning with the sopranos. Reverse the order and start with the lowest note first.
3. Write this chord on the board. Students identify it as a C major chord.
4. Play the C major scale on piano or bells.
5. Student writes the scale, note names, and the Roman numerals below each note.
6. Build the C chord on this scale. Lead the class to discover the chord structure (root, third, and fifth).

7. Students build the F(IV) and G(V) chords on the scale. Use the terms tonic, sub-dominant and dominant.

8. Play these chords on keyboard replicas and at the piano.

9. Add the number 7 to the G chord on the board, changing the G chord to the G_7.

10. Students discover how the addition of the 7 alters the chord.

C(I)   D   E   F(IV) G^7(V^7)   A   B   C

11. Can the students distinguish the difference in sound between a dominant chord and a dominant seventh chord?

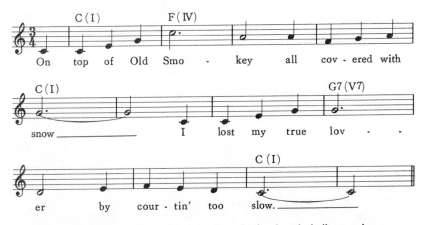

On top of Old Smo - key all cov - ered with snow_____ I lost my true lov - - er by cour - tin' too slow._____

1. After placing "Old Smokey" on the board, chord with bells, autoharp, or piano.

2. Students discover that three chords will be needed to accompany "Old Smokey."

3. Write C, F, and G_7 under another staff on the board.

4. Students volunteer individually to place on the staff any note from one of the three chords. Each student identifies his note and the chord to which it belongs.

5. The note placed on the staff is the name of the individual bell that the student takes back to his seat. The student now plays his bell when that particular chord occurs in the song.
   Autoharp rhythm: strum on "1"

$\frac{3}{4}$ ♩ 𝄾 𝄾 | ♩ 𝄾 𝄾 | ♩ 𝄾 𝄾 | etc.

Bells: play on "2, 3"

6. Try using the above procedure with "The More We Get Together," page 33.

MORE CHORDING EXPERIENCES

1. Sing, play, and notate the C major "Hello" chord.
2. Sing as a minor chord (changing the E to E flat) in both descending and ascending progression.
3. Students discover that a minor chord results when the third of the major chord is lowered a half-step. Notate.

— Sing and notate the following chords in like manner.

| Augmented | Diminished | Dom. 7th |

HALF STEP FORMULA

Students will be able to build chords at the piano starting on any note (root) of the scale if they know the half step sequence involved in the chord.

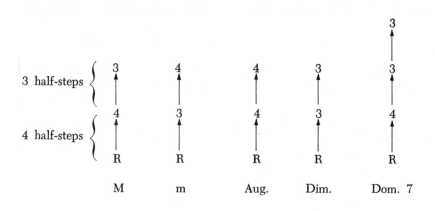

These chords are sometimes built by major thirds (four half steps) and minor thirds (three half steps).

NAME THAT CHORD GAME

A student plays one or more chords at the piano. Other students volunteer to identify these chords aurally. The student who has responded correctly takes his place at the piano and the game continues.

Inversions

1. Play piano chords in root position (either hand) to accompany "Old Smokey"; or, explain and play the following chord inversions:

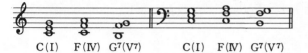

C(I)   F(IV)   G⁷(V⁷)   C(I)   F(IV)   G⁷(V⁷)

2. Play an "oom-pa-pa" accompaniment:

C(I)   F(IV)   G⁷ (V⁷)

Other Chord Uses

1. Review the familiar tonic triad.
2. Build and play chords of the ninth, eleventh, and thirteenth as follows:

3. Discuss the formation of these chords.
4. Play a series of thirteenth chords in sequence.

5. (Notice that the thirteenth chord contains all seven steps of the major scale.) Discuss the increase in volume, tension, and dissonance in these "skyscraper" chords.
6. Some chords in contemporary music are built on fourths or fifths rather than thirds. Play some examples for the class:

TONE CLUSTERS

Chords are often based upon a series of varied and unrelated intervals, as follows:

> — Indicate the note letter names in the above tone clusters as a student plays at the piano.

REMEMBER Singing, listening, playing, and identifying chords should be done frequently and over a period of time. It is by *repeated* listening and identification that students gain confidence regarding the harmonic element of music.

Remember also that at this age level, even a brief introduction to new harmonic sounds will broaden the musical horizons of many students.

Teaching Lessons

The following are lesson ideas for increasing the students' understanding of harmony in music. They involve many different types of activities, which emphasize the essential nature of music as an aural experience.

Second Movement (Exposition), SEVENTH SYMPHONY, Beethoven

This lesson involves listening for vertical as well as horizontal design. Emphasis should be placed on the harmonic nature of the chordal theme and the addition of a contrasting theme. This results in a type of polyphonic texture.

The following procedure includes the use of the overhead projecture, which has inspired the development of numerous teaching techniques. These techniques include the use of color, overlays, covering over parts of the transparency, etc., thus enabling the students to focus attention on designated aspects of the score. Combine several of these techniques in the presentation of the following lesson.

1. Isolate the top notes of the first theme. Discuss the absence of variety in both melody and rhythm.
2. Listen to a brief portion of the recording in order to discover the chordal structure of the first theme. Include a discussion of the low register, persistent rhythm, and minor mode.
3. Listen again to discover the addition of another theme and discuss the melodic characteristics such as register, melodic rhythm, phrasing, lyric line, etc.
4. Upon repeated listening of the entire A Section, discover the simultaneous development of both themes and the broadening effect caused by the dynamics and instrumentation.

HARMONIC FUNCTION

1. Sing "Kum Ba Yah."
2. Students learn the melody by rote.
3. Notate the melody on the board in the treble clef. Notate the melody in the bass clef.
4. Students play the melody on the piano.
5. Add a drum accompaniment. Before the voices enter, establish the rhythm by adding one drum at a time.

78

6. Try improvising other patterns for drum accompaniment.

Kum Ba Yah

African

Kum ba yah, my Lord, Kum ba yah. Kum ba yah, my Lord, Kum ba

yah. Kum ba yah my Lord, Kum ba yah. O Lord— Kum ba yah.

7. Sopranos sing a descant. Add the piano and/or bells.

Kum ba yah— etc.

O Lord,— Kum ba yah.

8. Try the alto melody and the soprano descant on one verse.

9. Discuss the polyphonic texture caused by the addition of the descant.

10. Play autoharp and/or piano chords.

C(I) G7(V7)

11. Experiment with bass harmony (chord roots) added to melody.

12. Sing by ear—the teacher indicates chord changes (I, IV, V) by hand levels and/or number of fingers.

13. Notate on the board.

14. Add alto-tenor harmony to the bass harmony and the melody.

15. Add a recorder part if desired.

Creating a Keyboard Accompaniment

Students derive many musical benefits from playing a keyboard accompaniment in class. This is especially true if they have derived the appropriate chord structure from their own knowledge and experience. It is wise, therefore, to present lessons of this type after students have some understanding of chords and their uses.

1. Sing "The Silvery Star" several times.

The Silvery Star

star of all the stars there was our star on - ly.

From *The Songster*, Cooperative Recreation Service. Used by permission. Harmonic variations from *Play!*, Monsour-Nelson, E. B. Marks. Used by permission.

2. Mark of eight measures on a staff. (Bass clef)
3. Write the chord symbol for each measure below the staff.
4. Write the chord notes in root position.
5. From the notes in each chord *derive* an accompaniment figure as in the example below. A student plays at the piano from the notation as the class sings the melody.

VARIATION 1

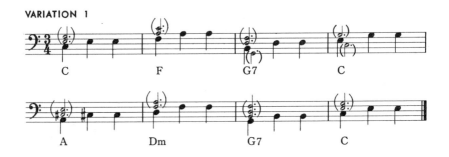

6. Derive the following variation. Discuss the process of derivation.

VARIATION 2

7. Encourage the students to experiment with additional variations.

Lessons in Miniature

1. "America."

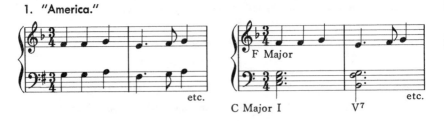

1. Play the melody of "America" in two different keys at once.
2. Play the melody in one key accompanied by chords in a different key.
3. Experiment with other key combinations. Some will sound more dissonant than others, for example E-flat and A.
4. Try other familiar melodies using the above procedure.

2. "Putnam's Camp" from *Three Places in New England*, Charles Ives (may be found in Bowmar Orchestral Library, *USA History*; and *Discovering Music Together*, Book 8, Follett.)

   1. While listening, discover the use of such familiar patriotic songs as "The British Grenadiers," "Hail Columbia," "Battle Cry of Freedom," and "Yankee Doodle."
   2. Also discover the use of polytonality and the purpose it serves to describe two street bands approaching and passing each other during a Fourth of July parade.

3. "Home on the Range," Cowboy tune

   ①   ②
   Oh give me a home where the buffalo roam,
   ①   ①
   Where the deer and the antelope play;
   ①   ②
   Where seldom is heard a discouraging word,
   ①   ③
   And the skies are not cloudy all day.

   ①   ①
   Home, home on the range
   ①   ①
   Where the deer and the antelope play;
   ①   ②
   Where seldom is heard a discouraging word,
   ①   ③
   And the skies are not cloudy all day.

1. Rid-ing a - long   2. Rid-ing a - long   3. Home on the range

— Using either a visual cue or hand signal, indicate the above harmony patterns to be sung with the melody. (The number of the pattern is indicated above the appropriate sections of the text.)

— Individual students may also give these harmonic directions "by ear."

— Add melodic instruments.

4. "Rocka My Soul," Spiritual

— Add harmony parts and sing in a rhythmic fashion.

— Students discover "by ear" the appropriate chords.

— Add autoharp accompaniment.

8

Understanding Tone Color

Tone producing instruments, including the voice, have distinct qualities of sound that constitute the element of tone color in music. These qualities, with all of their possible combinations, enable the composer to convey his musical intentions. Lessons on tone quality are important to the understanding of musical structure and especially to problems of musical communication and aural interpretation.

Students entering junior high school should have an adequate background for the comprehensive study of tone color. This study is best approached through lessons on the instruments of the band and orchestra, singing voices, folk instruments, keyboard instruments, and so forth. In junior high school, further work involves more complex tonal combinations as well as the fundamentals of tone production gained from the study of the acoustical properties of instruments. It is also desirable to learn the historical background of instruments as another avenue for the appreciation of aesthetic values inherent in all types of performing media and ensemble settings.

Even though some attention to tone quality is usually included in every musical experience, specific lessons should be presented which highlight this element. These lessons should include listening with visual charts, demonstrations of instruments, films, and so forth.

Teaching Lessons

BOLERO, Maurice Ravel

Ravel's "Bolero" contains many interesting tonal effects. Students enjoy listening for these particularly when the thematic and rhythmic structure remains constant as in the seventeen repetitions of the basic "Bolero" theme. Begin by motivating the students with a question such as the following: "If you were a composer limited to only one main theme, how would you develop an interesting musical composition for orchestra?" Next present the basic theme and accompanying rhythm given below. Discuss the structural step-wise character of the theme, and the repetitious nature of the rhythm.

BOLERO

Theme:

Ravel

Permission for reprint granted by Durand and Cie of Paris, France, Copyright Owners; Elkan-Vogel Co., Inc. of Philadelphia, Pa., Sole Agents.

1. Before listening to the *entire* composition, discuss several varieties of orchestral color appropriate for the theme and rhythm.
2. Listen all the way through for the more obvious solo instruments and combinations of instruments that play the theme.
3. Compare the tone color of each thematic repetition by selecting those that are similar and those that are different. Emphasize mood and effect.
4. Encourage students to use descriptive words (suggested by the color) to describe each repetition, such as "delicate," "somber," etc.
5. The following chart may be used by the teacher as a reference for the suggestions above or it may be given to the students as a visual aid. Students should *not* be expected to identify *all* of the instruments and combinations on this chart.

REMEMBER The primary purpose of instrumental identification and analysis should always be the increased understanding and enjoyment of the composition—not factual content as an end in itself.

1. Flute	2. Clarinet		3. Bassoon	4. Soprano Clarinet
5. Oboe	6. Flute, Trumpet		7. Tenor Saxophone	8. Soprano Saxophone
9. Piccolo, French Horn, Celesta		10. Oboe, English Horn, Clarinet		11. Trombone
12. Flute, Piccolo, Oboe, English Horn, Clarinet, Tenor Saxophone		13. Flute, Piccolo, Oboe Clarinet, Violin		
14. Flute, Piccolo, Oboe, English Horn, Clarinet, Tenor Saxophone, Violin		15. Flute, Piccolo, Oboe, English Horn, Trumpet, Violin		
16. Flute, Piccolo, Oboe, English Horn, Clarinet, Trombone, Soprano Saxophone, Violin, Viola, Cello		17. Flute, Piccolo, Oboe, Trumpet, Saxophone, Violin		
18. Flute, Piccolo, Oboe, Trumpet, Soprano and Tenor Saxophone, Violin				

"Mars" and "Neptune" from THE PLANETS by Gustav Holst

This suite is an interesting example of the varieties of tone color a composer can use to describe his ideas musically. The composition is scored for unusually large orchestra (two harps, six horns, four trumpets, six tympani, tenor tuba, celesta, and so forth). "Mars" and "Neptune" offer startling contrasts. Students are interested in the harsh, cruel sounds of "Mars" and the "outer space" feeling of "Neptune."[1]

[1]A lesson using the broad theme from "Jupiter" may be found in the chapter on "Understanding Melody."

1. Discuss the possible tone colors a composer could use to paint a musical picture of the planet Mars, the Bringer of War.

2. Listen to the composition and discover the extensive use of brass instruments, the use of dynamics and the relentless rhythm.

3. Discuss the possible tone colors a composer could use to paint a musical picture of Neptune, The Mystic.

4. Listen and discover that "Neptune" features strings, woodwinds, harps, and celesta. Also discover that Holst wrote only fragments of melody and that this is a wholly pianissimo movement.

5. Ask students what different tone color is added near the end. (Ladies' voices)

6. Discuss the effect created by the ladies' voices entering on a high G and also the long decrescendo at the end.

The following directions taken directly from the score may be of interest to the students. "The chorus is to be placed in an adjoining room, the door of which is to be left open until the last bar of the piece when it is to be slowly and silently closed."

These compositions also illustrate the varieties of tone colors possible on a single instrument. *Col legno* (playing on the wood of the violin bow) is used in the opening bars of "Mars." Tremolo and sordino (muted) violin is employed in "Neptune" as well as tremolo and glissando harp.

PAVANE POUR UNE INFANTE DEFUNTE, Ravel

1. Read the following poem to the class.

Lucy by William Wordsworth

She dwelt among the untrodden ways
  Beside the springs of Dove,
A maid whom there were none to praise
  And very few to love:
A violet by a mossy stone
  Half hidden from the eye!
Fair as a star, when only one,
  Is shining in the sky.
She lived unknown and few could know
  When Lucy ceased to be;
But she is in her grave and oh,
  The difference to me!

2. Listen to Ravel's composition: *"Pavane pour une infante défunte."*

3. Ask the students the following questions:
In what way is the poem related to the music? How is the mood of the poem achieved? How is the mood of the music achieved? How does the tone color in the music affect this mood? How does a painter achieve mood in a painting?

(This lesson was prepared by Sister Elizabeth Ann Compton, S. L., St. Mary's High School, Denver, Colorado).

CHANGING TONE COLOR

Contemporary composers have used tone color in many new ways. Traditionally one instrument or a group of instruments plays an entire phrase or melodic line. Since in contemporary style a different instrument is sometimes used for every note of a melody, the tone color and register also change frequently.

1. Sing "Swing Low" in traditional form.

2. Notate and play the following version, humming the melody throughout (notice the shifting register).

3. Finish the song, adding the students' ideas for changing tone color. Use other instruments that are available in the classroom.

SWING LOW

OTHER SUGGESTIONS

1. Listen to vocal recordings of male and female voices while noticing contrasts in tone color.

2. Listen to a choral rendition of "Finlandia" and compare it to the orchestral recording of "Finlandia" by Sibelius (chorale section).

3. Listen to a vocal recording of "Die Forelle" by Schubert and "Trout Quintette" by Schubert (Fourth Movement). Compare.

4. Listen to a piano version of "White Peacock" by Charles Griffes and the orchestral transcription by the composer of the same work.

5. Listen to recordings of non-western music such as *West Meets East*, Yehudi Menuhin and Ravi Shankar (Angel 36418). Discuss the interplay between

the sitar, violin, and drums in the composition entitled: "Shankar: Swara-Kakali."

6. Listen and compare two electronic compositions and discuss the distinctive qualities of sound which characterize each.[2]

List of Compositions Highlighting Instruments of the Orchestra

PICCOLO: *Beethoven*, Symphony No. 6 ("Pastoral"), Fourth Movement, "Storm."
Sousa, "Stars and Stripes Forever," trio.
Vivaldi, Concerto for Piccolo in A minor.
Ippolitoff-Ivanoff, "Caucasian Sketches," "Procession of the Sardar," First theme, piccolo and bassoon together.

FLUTE: *Dvorak*, Symphony No. 5 (From the "New World"), First Movement, Second theme.
Mozart, Flute Concerto in G major.
Griffes, Poem for Flute and Orchestra.
Tchaikovsky, Nutcracker Suite, "Dance of the Flutes."
Saint-Saens, Carnival of the Animals, "Birds."

CLARINET: *Tchaikovsky*, Symphony No. 5, Introduction.
Sibelius, Symphony No. 1, Introduction.
Mozart, Clarinet Quintet in A major.
Gershwin, "Rhapsody in Blue," beginning.

OBOE: *Tchaikovsky*, Symphony No. 4, Second Movement, First theme.
Schubert, Symphony No. 7 in C major (Great), Second Movement, First theme (after introduction).
Mozart, Oboe Quartet in F major.
Beethoven, Symphony No. 3 ("Eroica"), Second Movement, First theme.

ENGLISH HORN: *Dvorak*, Symphony No. 5 (From the "New World"), Second Movement.
Franck, Symphony in D minor, Second Movement, First theme (after introduction).
Rossini, William Tell Overture, "Calm."

BASSOON: *Tchaikovsky*, Symphony No. 6 ("*Pathetique*"), Introduction.

[2]Excellent suggestions for presenting electronic music may be found in *Making Music Your Own*, Book 8, Silver Burdett Co., 1968; and *Discovering Music Together*, Book 8, Follett Pub. Co.

Rimsky-Korsakov, Scheherazade, Second
Movement, (after introduction).
Mozart, Bassoon Concerto in B.
Dukas, Sorcerer's Apprentice, "Broom"
theme.

FRENCH *Tchaikovsky*, Symphony No. 5, Second Movement,
HORN: First theme.
Beethoven, Symphony No. 3 (*"Eroica"*),
Third Movement (Trio section).
Mendelssohn, "Nocturne" from A Midsummer
Night's Dream.
Strauss, R., Till Eulenspiegel's Merry
Pranks, "Till" theme.

TRUMPET: *Purcell-Clark*, Trumpet Voluntary in D
major.
Tchaikovsky, "Capriccio italien," beginning.
Haydn, Trumpet Concerto in E-Flat.

TROMBONE: *Liszt*, Les Preludes, Second section:
"Andante Maestoso."
Wagner, Tannhauser Overture, "Pilgrim's"
theme.

TUBA: *Berlioz*, Symphonie Fantastique, "Dies
Irae," theme, Fifth Movement.

HARP: *Tchaikovsky*, Nutcracker Suite, "Waltz
of the Flowers."
Mozart, Concerto for Flute and Harp.

CELESTA: *Tchaikovsky*, Nutcracker Suite, "Dance
of the Sugar Plum Fairy."

TIMPANI: *Haydn*, Symphony No. 103 (Drum Roll)
Introduction.
Wagner, Die Gotterdammerung, Funeral
Music, beginning.
Grofé, Grand Canyon Suite, Introduction.

VIOLIN: *Rimsky-Korsakov*, Scheherazade, Third
Movement, First theme.
Haydn, Symphony No. 104, (London), Second
Movement, First theme.
Beethoven, Sonata for Violin and Piano in
F major (Spring).
Mendelssohn, Concerto for Violin in E minor.
Paganini, "Moto Perpetuo."

VIOLA: *Telemann*, Viola Concerto in G major.
Mozart, Duos for Violin and Viola.
Tchaikovsky, Marche Slav.
Berlioz, Harold in Italy.

CELLO AND STRING BASS:	*Schubert*, Symphony No. 8 (*"Unfinished"*). First Movement. *Brahms*, Cello Sonata in F Major. *Saint-Saens*, Carnival of the Animals, "Elephant."
WOODWIND GROUP:	*Tchaikovsky*, Symphony No. 4, Third Movement. *Brahms*, Variations on a Theme by Haydn, beginning. *Wagner, Die Meistersinger*, "Prelude."
BRASS GROUP:	*Sibelius*, Finlandia, beginning. *Tchaikovsky*, Symphony No. 4, Third Movement, Third theme. *Wagner, Lohengrin*, Prelude to Act III. *Moussorgsky-Ravel*, Pictures at an Exhibition, "Great Gate at Kiev."
STRING GROUP:	*Mozart*, Eine kleine Nachtmusik. *Barber*, Adagio for Strings.
PERCUSSION GROUP:	*Chavez*, Toccata for Percussion. *Reed*, La Fiesta Mexicana, "Mass." *Kodaly*, Harry Janos Suite, "Viennese Musical Clock."
GENERAL:	*First Chair* (Philadelphia Orchestra) Columbia. *Young Person's Guide to the Orchestra*, Britten. *Instruments of the Orchestra*, Vanguard. *Instruments of the Orchestra*, RCA–LES6000. *Music Educators Series: Percussion*, Capitol HBR21003.

9

Understanding Form

"Architects work with forms. They start with lines which, when used in certain ways create squares, triangles, rectangles, which in turn create rooms, which in turn may result in a house of certain design. So, too, music deals with forms. . . . Form is the agent by which order is given to art, thus making it more easily grasped."[1] (WILLIAM HUGH MILLER)

The manner in which melodic, rhythmic, and harmonic materials are developed constitutes the form of a particular piece of music. For this reason the study of musical form can be one of the more interesting facets of the music class. When it is presented in a stimulating fashion, students will derive considerable pleasure from listening for form. They will usually enjoy detecting the imaginative devices composers employ to achieve unity and variety, repetition and contrast.

The study of form should coincide with lessons in melody, rhythm, and harmony. This supposes that teachers will relate the definitive elements of form to songs, recordings, and other activities.

Unity and Variety

— Play the following examples. Ask students to describe the way in which each element has altered the main idea.

MAIN IDEA

[1]*Introduction to Music Appreciation* (New York: Chilton Company, 1961), p. 167.

TONALITY (MODE) CHANGED

MELODY AND RHYTHM CHANGED

COUNTER-MELODY ADDED

REGISTER LOWERED

RHYTHM CHANGED

HARMONY CHANGED

— Discuss other ways in which the main idea could have been altered such as register, texture, countermelody, etc.

— Play the following examples of achieving variety. Students should describe each alteration.

Ach Du Lieber Augustin

MAIN IDEA

MELODY SAME, HARMONY CHANGED

With permission of the publishers from *What to Listen for in Music* by Aaron Copland. Copyright © 1939, 1957 by the McGraw-Hill Book Company, Inc.

MELODY CHANGED, HARMONY SAME

MELODY SAME, REGISTER CHANGED, COUNTERMELODY ADDED

RHYTHM CHANGED, HARMONY CHANGED

MELODY SAME, TEXTURE ADDED

FOLLOW UP Mozart Variations (page 50); Ballantine, *Variations on Mary Had A Little Lamb*; Dohnanyi, *Variations on a Nursery Theme*; Handel, *Suite No. 5 in E Major* (Fourth Movement); Alec Templeton, *Variations on Farmer in the Dell* (Riserside Wonderland 1403); Haydn, *Surprise Symphony* (Second Movement)

Repetition and Contrast

1. Play and sing "Greensleeves."
2. Ask students to discover the number and repetition of melodies within the song.
3. Chart the form.

GREENSLEEVES (AA' BB')

A

A'

B

B'

FOLLOW UP "America" (AB); "Oh, Susanna" (AA'BA'); "For the Beauty of the Earth" (AAB); "Dance of the Flutes" from *The Nutcracker Suite* (ABA'CC'A); "Lift Thine Eyes" from *Elijah* (ABA').

Another rewarding experience is the discovery that some forms of jazz are actually improvisations on a theme.

Teaching Lessons

APPALACHIAN SPRING, Aaron Copland

Teach lessons which explore other means of variety and contrast such as register, sonority, orchestral timbre, texture, augmentation, imitation, and instrumental color as they apply to the *Appalachian Spring* setting (Aaron Copland) of "Simple Gifts."

Violins, Muted Horns

Low *f*
Strings

FIFTH ENTRANCE

Tutti

Copyright 1946 by Hawkes & Son (London) Ltd. Reprinted by permission.

1. Play and sing the alteration of pitches in the development of the melody. (Encircled in the score.)

2. Notice the augmentation of the rhythm.

LITTLE FUGUE IN G MINOR, Bach

There are many large forms *of* music which students in junior high school should study, such as sonata-allegro, rondo, fugue, theme and variations, etc. The following are teaching suggestions for the study of the fugue.

The fugue form may be introduced by singing rounds, canons, and simultaneous melodies.[2]

Little Fugue in G Minor

SUBJECT   Bach

[2]Teaching lessons using "Little Fugue in G Minor," may be found in *Growing With Music*, Book 8, Prentice-Hall, Inc.; and *Discovering Music Together*, Book 8, Follett Pub. Co.

COUNTERSUBJECT

1. Acquaint the students with brief background information on Bach's *Little Fugue in G Minor*. The fugue is a form of counterpoint that was perfected in the musical genius of J. S. Bach. This fugue was written between 1708 and 1717 while Bach was the organist at Weimar, Germany. It is called the *Little Fugue in G Minor* to distinguish it from a later fugue which was longer and more complicated—the *Great Fugue in G Minor*.

2. Acquaint students with the principal melody or subject before they attempt to listen to the fugue. Use an organ recording if possible.

QUESTIONS FOR STUDENT DISCOVERY

1. What chord is outlined by the first three notes of the subject? (G minor chord)
   How does the rhythm of the subject progress?

2. Follow the order in which the four voices enter. Identify these four voices. (Subject is first stated in the soprano voice, next by the alto voice four tones lower, then by the tenor voice an octave below the soprano, and finally by the bass an octave below the alto.)

3. Is the subject always stated in minor? (Two statements are in B-flat major.)

4. How many times is the subject stated? (Nine times)

5. Listen. Discover the countersubject. (When the alto voice enters, the countersubject is stated by the soprano, etc.)

6. Does the fugue begin and end in the same tonality? (Ends in G major. Discuss the Picardy third.)

   MUSICAL TERMS Fugue; Counterpoint; Subject; Countersubject; Picardy third.

PASSACAGLIA IN C MINOR, Bach

The title of this form comes from the combination of two Spanish words "passar" (to walk) and "calle" (street). In musical terms, however, it consists of a repeated theme (similar to an "ostinato") while a series of variations is played above it. In this particular passacaglia, there are twenty interesting variations above a clearly stated bass theme.

1. Sing the above theme several times to establish the sound securely in the students' memory.
2. Listen to the exposition of the theme on a recording and discuss the register, and any appropriate melodic characteristics.
3. Now listen to the variations, noting the differences among them. Emphasize the contrasts and effects the organ is able to produce with each variation.

CREATING A RONDO

For variety, approach the study of form from the discovery of repetition and contrast. The following is a suggested procedure using the Rondo form ABACA given only the charted form as a clue.

1. Teacher puts the letters ABACA on the board, chart or overhead projector.
2. Students discover the repetition of the A theme.
3. Teacher explains the characteristics of Rondo form via repetition and contrast.
4. Given a simple rhythm pattern for the A section, students create B and C sections resulting in a rhythm rondo. Accompany with some type of physical response. Add instruments.
5. Try creating rondos combining melodies and rhythms.
6. Follow up with listening lessons:

    "Col. Bogey"—Alford (*Music USA*—Bowmar), ABACA

    The Plow that Broke the Plains, "Cattle" Thomson (*Music USA*—Bowmar), ABACABAC

    "Eine kleine Nachtmusik," "Romanza," Mozart, ABACA

    "Introduction and Rondo Capriccioso (violin and orchestra) Saint-Saens, ABACABA

    "Prelude III"—Gershwin, ABACA

10

Relating Content

Music should be approached by participation in many musical activities through which students learn the elements common to most types of music, i.e., melody, rhythm, harmony, and form. These elements will guide students to the primary objective of the class—musical knowledge and appreciation.

Even though the elements of music may be separated for the temporary purposes of study and perception, they are always related within a musical composition. For this reason, considerable attention should be given to the elements as they affect the totality of a musical idea.

REMEMBER Do not allow your class to degenerate into a series of routine lessons in facts and skills. Music is inspiring because of its artistic ingredients. Keep this in mind when planning the content of all your lessons.

Designing Lessons with a Plan

Just as a good work of art contains unity and variety, so should a music lesson. Design lessons that lead directly toward the established objectives and outcomes of the class. Don't allow the class period to consist of a series of unrelated activities which have no recognizable sequence of musical growth. The following suggested plans may help.

FUGUES FOR TEENAGERS

Teenagers usually have numerous experiences with counterpoint through the singing of rounds, canons, simultaneous melodies, and descants. Because of this background, the study of fugues, both instrumental and choral, generally proves to be an exciting discovery of a new musical form. It is doubtful that the students should become too absorbed in the highly technical details of the fugue. Perhaps an understanding of the general characteristics of this form and the ability to hear the entrance of the voices, following them through to their exciting climax, is sufficient at this age. This unit will also afford students an opportunity to learn about the organ and harpsichord—two early instruments for which fugues were composed.

RECORDINGS[1]

Round and Round (Young Peoples Records)

Cat's Fugue, Scarlatti (harpsichord)

Johann Sebastian Bach, His Story and His Music (VOX MM 3500)

Little Fugue in G Minor, Bach (Organ recording; Stokowski and/or Cailliet transcription for orchestra)

Great Fugue in G Minor, Bach

"Switched-on-Bach" (Moog Synthesizer), Columbia MS 7194

Young Persons' Guide to the Orchestra, Britten

"Pumpkin Eater's Fugue," McBride from recording *Teen Scenes,* (CRI 119) and *Music U.S.A.* (Bowmar)

Vocal and instrumental examples of fugal and canonic treatment of a melody within the structure of a composition.

Appalachian Spring, Copland (see pp. 95–96)

"For Unto Us A Child Is Born," Handel (*Messiah*)

Semper Fidelis, March, Sousa (see page 34)

Jupiter Symphony, Fourth Movement, Mozart

Symphony for Band, Third Movement, Hindemith

Music for Strings, Percussion, and Celesta, Bartók (beginning section)

"Il était une bergère," *Folk Songs of the Old World,* Vol. 2, Wagner Chorale, Capitol P8388

Bach, Vol. 1, Albert Schweitzer, organist, Columbia (ML 4600)

Prelude and Fugue in Jazz, Press (RCA, LSC 2789)

Bach's Greatest Hits, Swingle Singers (Philips 200-097)

"Fugue and Chorale on Yankee Doodle," Virgil Thomson, Bowmar Orchestral Library (Music USA).

FILMS AND FILMSTRIPS

Bach, Johann Sebastian, Filmstrip (EBF); *Bach,* (Bowmar)

Instruments of the Orchestra, "Variations and Fugue on a Theme of Purcell," Britten (BIS)

Iturbi, José, Harpsichord (Mills)

---

[1]These recordings include choral and instrumental fugues as well as fugal and canonic treatment within the confines of larger forms.

Landowska, Wanda, Harpsichord (EBF)
Little Fugue in G Minor (TFC)
Music for Young People: The Elements of Composition (Indiana University)
Music in the Wind, shorter version of *Singing Pipes* (Can NFB)
Musical Form Series: The Fugue (NET)
Singing Pipes, organ building and Bach's "Toccata and Fugue in D Minor"
   (Can NFB)
Toccata and Fugue in D Minor, Bryce Canyon setting (Avis)

SONGS TO SING

Rounds
Canons:
   "Ol' Texas"
   "Panis Angelicus"
   "All Creatures of Our God and King"
Songs that can be sung simultaneously:
   "Three Blind Mice" and "Are You Sleeping?"
   "Skip to My Lou" and "Ten Little Indians"
   "Keep the Home Fires Burning" and "There's A Long, Long, Trail"
   Partner Songs, Beckman, Frederick. Boston: Ginn, 1958.
   More Partner Songs, Beckman, Frederick. Boston: Ginn, 1960.

RELATED READINGS

Goss, Madeleine, *Deep Flowing Brook: The Story of Johann Sebastian Bach.*
   New York: Holt, 1938.
Mirsky, Reba Paeff, *Johann Sebastian Bach*, Chicago: Follett, 1965.
Wheeler, Opal, and Sybil Deucher, *Curtain Calls for Joseph Haydn and
   Sebastian Bach*. New York: Dutton, 1939.
Wheeler, Opal, and Sybil Deucher, *Sebastian Bach: The Boy From Thuringia*.
   New York: Dutton, 1937.

REFERENCES FOR THE TEACHER

Bernstein, Leonard, *The Joy of Music*, pp. 225–65. New York: Simon &
   Schuster, 1959.
Hartshorn, William C., and Helen S. Leavitt, *The Pilot*, pp. 65–74. Boston:
   Ginn, 1940.
Schweitzer, Albert, *J. S. Bach*, Vols. 1 and 2. New York: MacMillan, 1935.
Tipton, Gladys, and Eleanor Tipton, *Adventures in Music*, Teachers Guide,
   VI, Vol. 1, pp. 26–33. New York: RCA, 1960.

REFERENCES FOR THE STUDENT

Bauer, Marion, and Ethel Peyser, *How Music Grew*, pp. 244–54. New York:
   Putnam, 1925.
Britten, Benjamin, and Imogene Holst, *The Wonderful World of Music*,
   pp. 46–47. New York: Doubleday, 1958.

Buchanan, Fannie, and Charles Luckenbill, *How Man Made Music*, rev. ed., pp. 174–186. Chicago: Follett, 1959.

Hartshorn, William C., and Helen S. Leavitt, *Prelude*, pp. 84–93. Boston: Ginn, 1940.

Sandved, K. B., et al., eds. *The World of Music*, London: Waverly Book Company, 1954.

SUGGESTED ACTIVITIES AND PROCEDURES

1. Sing rounds, canons, and songs that can be sung simultaneously.

2. Chant and play rhythm rounds on appropriate rhythm instruments. (For examples of rhythm rounds see pages 44 and 63).

3. Present a listening lesson on *Little Fugue in G. Minor*. (See page 96.

4. Contrast organ recording of *Little Fugue in G Minor* with orchestral transcriptions of Stokowski and/or Cailliet.

5. Contrast Bach's fugues with McBride's "Fugato on a Well-Known Theme" and "Pumpkin Eater's Fugue."

6. Interpret a fugue with bodily movement.

7. Discuss the life of Albert Schweitzer and his great contributions in the fields of medicine, philosophy, theology, and music.

8. Listen to a recording of Albert Schweitzer playing Bach's music.

9. Use films and filmstrips to increase understanding of counterpoint, fugue, organ, harpsichord, and J. S. Bach.

10. Encourage students to give short oral reports on the lives of the various composers studied.

11. Attend an organ concert in which a fugue is performed.

12. Have piano students prepare and play examples of fugues (both classical and contemporary) for the class.

13. Prepare a bulletin board.

14. Compare examples of Baroque art and architecture with Bach's music.

15. Derive appropriate musical terms from the study of the fugue.

Ideas in a Nutshell

Lists of materials are most useful within a framework of reference. Unless the teacher is familiar with the publication of selections on a particular list, the list itself is of little practical value. Brief suggestions and ideas for lessons involving materials and activities are given below.

MATERIALS

Record:	*Songs of the West,* Norman Luboff Choir (Columbia CL 657)	Sing these western songs. Contrast the simple folk song quality with the sophisticated recorded arrangement of the same tune.
Songs:	"Colorado Trail" "Streets of Laredo" "Old Chisholm Trail," and others	
Song:	"The Trout," Schubert	Sing the song and discover the
Record:	"Quintet in A Major," op. 114, "Trout." Schubert, (4th Movement)	characteristics of the melody. Listen and discuss the variations of the "trout" theme in the fourth move-
Film:	*Schubert and His Music* (Coronet)	ment of the quintet. Also, compare the standard quintet instrumentation with that of *this* quintet which is piano, violin, viola, cello, and bass. Compare the programmatic aspects of "The Linden Tree" from the film with "The Trout."
Record:	*Frank Sinatra Conducts Tone Poems of Color* (Capitol W 735)	Select three contrasting colors. Read the poem introducing each color. Identify the color after listening to
Poems:	Record jacket	the record (melody, harmony, instrumentation, and rhythm will aid the students in identification). Plan a bulletin board using these colors.
Record:	*The Music Man,* Meredith Willson (original cast) (Capitol WA 0990)	Acquaint the students with the story and music of *The Music Man.* Sing "Seventy-Six Trombones" and
Songs:	"Seventy-Six Trombones" "Goodnight, My Someone"	"Goodnight, My Someone." Point out that Meredith Willson used the same melody for both of these songs.
Records:	*Pacific 231,* Honegger *Little Train of Caipira,* Villa-Lobos	Unit on transportation Unit on program music Contrast the music of the large,
Songs:	"Pat on the Railroad" "I've Been Workin' On The Railroad"	heavy steam engine of *Pacific 231* with the little mountain train of Brazil.
Film:	*Pacific 231* (Young America)	Compare the musical elements in each setting. If the film is shown before the record is played, have the students write their reactions to the audio and visual aspects of the film.
Record:	*Pomp and Circumstance No. 1,* Elgar	Listen to the recording. Discover the derivation of the song
Song:	"Land of Hope and Glory"	from the Trio section of this well-known composition.

Record:	*The Happy Wanderer and Other Songs,* Obernkirchen Children's Choir (Angel 65038)	Sing "The Happy Wanderer" in English and/or German. Listen to it sung in German. Read translations of other songs from the recording for students. The class may be interested in learning some of these songs in German.
Records: Songs:	*Gaîté Parisienne,* Offenbach "Tortoises" (*Carnival of the Animals*), Saint-Saëns "Can Can" (*Pop Hits from the Classics*), Ted Heath and Orchestra (London LL 3124) "Can Can" and "Buffalo Gals." Beckman, Frederick, *Partner Songs.* Boston: Ginn, 1958.	Sing the partner songs, "Can Can" and "Buffalo Gals." Discover the "Can Can" melody in *Gaîté Parisienne.* Discover Saint-Saëns' humorous treatment of the same melody. Contrast these versions with the Ted Heath jazz arrangement.
Record: Libretto: Book:	*Amahl and the Night Visitors,* Menotti (original cast) (RCA LM 1701) *Amahl and the Night Visitors,* Menotti. New York: G. Schirmer Menotti, Gian-Carlo, *Amahl and the Night Visitors.* New York: McGraw-Hill, 1952.	Listen to this contemporary one-act opera as students follow librettos. Good introduction to opera.
Records: Film Strip: Books:	*Stars and Stripes Forever,* Sousa *Semper Fidelis,* Sousa *Washington Post,* Sousa *John Philip Sousa* (VOX MM 3620) *John Philip Sousa* (EBF) Sousa, John P., *Marching Along.* Eau Claire, Wisc.: Hale, 1941. Lingg, Ann, *John Philip Sousa.* New York: Holt, 1954.	Unit on "Here Comes the Band" Unit on the "March King" See the listening lesson on *Semper Fidelis,* page 34. Indicate that "Semper Fidelis" is the motto of the United States Marine Corps and that the *Washington Post March* was often selected as music for the two-step, a popular dance of the early 1900's.
Records: Songs:	Excerpts from *H. M. S. Pinafore.* D'Oyly Carte Opera Company, Gilbert and Sullivan (London LL 809) Complete Recording of *H. M. S. Pinafore* "We Sail the Ocean Blue" "I Am the Captain of the Pinafore" "When I was a Lad"	Teacher reads or tells the story of *H. M. S. Pinafore,* playing recorded excerpts as they appear in the plot. Learn some of the better-known songs. If the class is interested, listen to a complete recording of the operetta. Write and dramatize a short version of *H. M. S. Pinafore,* using songs within the students' vocal ranges. Plan an *H. M. S. Pinafore* bulletin

Books:	Wheeler, Opal, *H. M. S. Pinafore*. New York: Dutton, 1940.	board displaying pupils' art work of the ship and the characters in the operetta.
	Hyatt, M., and W. Fabell, *Gilbert and Sullivan Song Book*. New York: Random House, 1955.	Assign book reports on outside reading.
	Power-Waters, Alma S., *Melody Maker* (Life of Sir Arthur Sullivan). New York: Dutton, 1959.	

Record:	*Alec Templeton's Children's Concert* (Riverside Wonderland 1403) Variations on "Farmer in the Dell" "17th Century Gigue" "Academic Festival Overture" "Mazurka" "Mambo" "Real Cool"	Use these variations to follow up "Dances New–Dances Old" p. 43.

Records:	*Sound of Music*, Rodgers and Hammerstein (original cast) (Columbia KOL 5450)	Familiarize students with the story of the Trapp family. Listen to the recording of the Rodgers and Hammerstein musical
Songs:	"Do-Re-Mi" "The Sound of Music" "The Lonely Goatherd" "Climb Every Mountain"	show based on their story. Sing the songs. See the movie.
Book:	Trapp, Maria, *Story of the Trapp Family Singers*. Philadelphia: Lippincott, 1949.	
Film:	*The Sound of Music* (Century-Fox)	

Records:	*Mississippi Suite*, Ferde Grofé *Mark Twain Tonight*, Hal Holbrook (Columbia OL 5440)	Integrate Mark Twain's literature with Holbrook's exciting impersonation and Grofé's musical description of the Mississippi River.
Books:	Twain, Mark, *Huckleberry Finn* Twain, Mark, *Life on the Mississippi*	Sing "Daybreak," which is based on the principal melody in Mardi Gras.
Song:	"Daybreak"	

Record:	"Fantasia on Greensleeves," Vaughan Williams	Sing the songs. Discover the techniques that Vaughan
Songs:	"Greensleeves" "What Child Is This?"	Williams used in this fantasia on a well-known theme.

Record:	*Sounds of New Music* (Folkways 6160)	Develop a unit on sound. Discuss the contribution of science

Film:	*Looking at Sounds* (BIF, McGraw-Hill)	to present-day musical life.
Books:	*Making Music Your Own*, Book 7, pp. 1–4; and *Discovering Music Together*, Book 8, pp. 178–179.	Plan a trip to a local music store for demonstrations of high fidelity and stereophonic sound.
Records:	"Fugue in C minor from Well-Tempered Clavier, Book 1. Fugue in C minor as found on recording *Bach's Greatest Hits*, Swingle Singers (Philips, PHM 200-097). Switched-on-Bach" (Moog Synthesizer), Columbia MS 7194.	Unit on Bach. The Fugue, or Jazz. Discover that the use of voices and the added rhythm section is what makes Bach "swing."
Record: Filmstrip:	*Rodeo*, Copland *Rodeo* (color) SE 8036 Education Audio Visual, Inc., 26 Marble Ave., Pleasantville, N. Y.	View the filmstrip while listening to the accompanying record. (Pictures for "Buckaroo Holiday" and "Corral Nocturne" are actual photographs of present day rodeos and ranch scenes. Pictures for "Saturday Night Waltz" and "Hoe Down" are from productions of the ballet by the Ballet Russe and American Ballet Theater). Listen to other compositions by this composer. Encourage students to illustrate the music.
Song: Record: Book: Film:	"The Gypsy Forge," *Birchard Music Series*, Book 7, p. 58. *Hungarian Dance No. 6*, Brahms (Bowmar Orchestral Library, #62). Deucher, Sybil, *The Young Brahms*. New York: Dutton, 1949. Brahms and His Music (Coronet, 1957).	Sing the song. Listen to the recording to discover the orchestral setting of the melody via the alternating of pitch and rhythm. Discuss the form. Relate to the background information provided by the book and film to the music.
Recordings: Songs:	"The Erl King," Schubert "The Trout," Schubert (Vienna Choir, Philips 900-002) *Art Songs for Treble Voices*. Arranged by Marguerite Hood. New York, Mills Music, Inc. 1965.	Listen to the "Erl King" and discover how the melody and accompaniment reflect the meaning of the text. Listen to the recording of "The Trout" as sung by a member of the Vienna Boys Choir. Sing several art songs.

Appendix A:
The Music Classroom

"The function of the music classroom is to produce music."

Recommendations

An adequate classroom should have the following facilities.

— size determined by the largest group you teach—probably chorus
— large room wider than it is deep
— 260 cubic feet per student in addition to adequate space in front of the room for piano, desk, filing cabinet, phonograph, and class activities
— unilateral lighting (windows on one side of room) and adequate artificial lighting
— semicircular permanent risers
— ample well-placed blackboard space (some with permanently lined music staves)
— two bulletin boards
— adequate storage space, with locks, for all supplies and materials
— proper acoustical construction
— good ventilation
— temperature 68 to 70 degrees
— good structural insulation
— closet for teacher
— location near stage if used also for chorus and other performing groups

The auditorium, the cafeteria, the cafetorium, or the gymnasium *cannot* be recommended for a vocal classroom. Some disadvantages of such areas would be:

— immensity of space
— improper lighting
— poor ventilation
— inadequate blackboard and bulletin board space
— lack of teacher's desk, arm chairs, storage space, etc.

— probability of its not being acoustically treated for light voices

— difficulty of orderly and consistent seating plan

— class disruption and scheduling conflicts with other school activities

Are other comparable academic programs conducted in the auditorium or cafeteria?

Equipment, Supplies, and Materials

EQUIPMENT

— small size piano and bench

— teacher's desk and chair

— tablet arm chairs for students (drop desk arms only if room is also used for instrumental groups)

— phonograph and radio

— tape recorder available in the school

— overhead projector

— filing cabinet(s)

— wall maps

— screen for film projector

— dark curtains for windows

— outlets at both front and back of the room

— record cabinets if records are not stored in storage closet

INSTRUCTIONAL SUPPLIES

— staff paper for student use

— manuscript paper

— duplicator staff-lined masters

— overhead transparencies

— chart size staff-lined paper

— variety of colored construction paper (18" x 24" size for bulletin boards)

— plastic bulletin board letters (Micro Sign Pin Back Letters, Display Pin Back Numbers, Gaylord Library Supply, Riverside, California)

— school room seating plan: available from school supply companies

— staff liner

— colored chalk

— felt pens in various colors

— notator

— flannel board and musical symbols

TEACHING MATERIALS

— at least one set of song books for each grade 7, 8, and 9 (one book per student)

— one set of community-type song books

— recordings (representative of periods, composers, instruments, vocal, etc.)
— recordings to accompany song texts, if available
— autoharp (one or more) and case
— rhythm instruments (drums, claves, maracas, etc.)
— song bells (preferably individual bells)
— assortment of instruments such as ukuleles, recorders, etc.
— books about music—usually in library
— photographs (of instruments, composers, and performers)
— materials of musical interest clipped from newspapers, magazines, etc.
— keyboard replicas[1]
— autoharp charts
— musical scores

A bulletin board which was the outgrowth of a unit on the piano.

The Teacher and the Music Classroom

— The general appearance and atmosphere of the music room should reflect the subject you teach—MUSIC.
— Keep the classroom clean and orderly.
— Keep the chairs straightened and the floor picked up. (Is the custodian your friend?)
— Catalog the record collection—keep records clean, in jackets, and stored properly. Chalk dust is especially harmful to records.

[1]Shop classes sometimes undertake the making of wooden, raised keyboards as a project.

— Store books in an orderly fashion to prevent unnecessary damage and confusion when distributing materials.

— Check the phonograph needle often.

— Keep the piano and autoharp in good tune at all times.

— Store rhythm instruments in a convenient location.

— Arrange and file bulletin board materials.

— Change the bulletin board at least once a month.

— Before closing the door—STOP—Are the lights off? Is the record player still on?

ENCOURAGE RESPECT FOR MUSICAL EQUIPMENT

In a junior high school, a new grand piano was purchased for the auditorium stage. In order to instill in the student body a respect for this fine new instrument, the following procedure took place.

— Music classes were taken to the stage and "introduced" to the new member of the school.

— The students in the music classes did library research, followed by oral reports on the ancestors of the modern piano, the history of the piano, famous composers for the piano, and famous performing pianists. Recordings were used for illustration.

— Students were taken to a nearby music school for a demonstration of the virginal, the clavichord, and the harpsichord.

— A display was prepared for the bulletin board in the main hall of the school building.

— An assembly program was the climax of the project. It included reports by music class members, piano solos by junior high school students, and a solo by an accomplished alumnus.

Many school libraries allow students to check out recordings for home listening. Students especially like those recordings that have been presented in class.

Appendix B: Part Songs
for Changing Voices

Examples of harmony songs which fit the vocal ranges usually found in seventh and eighth grades follow, and are included here for reference and study.

Once More, My Soul

Andante
mp

American Folk Hymn

1. Once more, my soul, the rising day Salutes thy waking eyes; Once more, my voice, thy tribute pay To Him that rules the skies.
2. Night unto night His Name repeats, The day renews the sound; Wide as the heav'n on which He sits, To turn the seasons round.

Thanks Be To Thee

Marie Schmidt

George Frederick Handel

for this har-vest sea - son; our ___ songs we

raise. Grate - ful - ly we lift our voic-es now___ and to

Thee we give praise.

D.C. al Fine

dim.

Earth, Rejoice

Traditional Carol
(Adapted by William S. Haynie)

Con spirito

1. While shep-herds watched their flocks by night, Sud - den -ly came an
2. "Fear not," the an - gel said to them, "Je - sus is born in
3. Wise men did come from lands a - far, Led to the man - ger

an - gel bright.
Beth-le - hem." O Earth, re-joice! Earth, re-joice! Christ is born! Christ is born!
by a star.

Joy to the world! Al - le - lu - ia! Joy to the world! Al - le - lu - ia!

Sicilian Hymn

Arranged by Catherine Ann Cook

O Sanc - tis - si - ma,— O pi - is - si - ma,—

Dul - cis Vir - go Ma - ri - a.

Ma - ter a - ma - ta in - te - me - ra - ta

O - ra, O - ra pro - no - bis.

Interlochen Press for "Sicilian Hymn" by Catherine Ann Cook. Used by permission.

Blow the Man Down

American Sea Chanty

1. Come___ all   ye young fel - lows that fol - low the sea
2. A - board   the Black Ball - er   I   first served my time With a
3. There were tin - kers and tail - ors and sail - ors and all

And please pay at - ten - tion and
yo - ho! We'll blow the man down, And   on   the Black Ball - er   I
That shipped for good sea - men on

lis - ten to me
wast - ed my time   Give us some time to blow the man down.
board the Black Ball

Michael, Row the Boat Ashore

Easy Bounce

Arranged by Tom Patrick

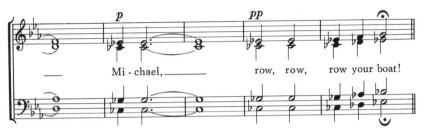

Mi - chael, _____ row, row, row your boat!

Arranged by Tom Patrick, Catalina High School, Tucson, Arizona. Used by permission.

Appendix C:

Weekly Lesson Blank

	Mon.	Tues.	Wed.	Thurs.	Fri.
Songs New and Old					
Rhythms					
Chording and Part Work					
Listening					
Playing Instruments					
Creative Composition					
Enrichment					

Appendix D:
Criteria for Selecting
Music Textbooks

	*1	2	3	4

- Will the song material appeal to adolescents?
- Are the vocal ranges appropriate?
- Do the accompaniments enhance the beauty of the songs?
- Are there sufficient songs of lasting value?
- Do the vocal arrangements allow parts other than the soprano to sing the melody?
- Is there sufficient variety of song material?
- Are there several interesting part songs which can be learned easily and quickly?
- Are there some part songs which would challenge your most musical group?
- Is there an ample supply of:
    Descants
    Rounds
    Canons
    Optional harmonic parts
    Keyboard experiences
- Are there provisions for the use of orchestral instruments?
- What is the calibre of the listening material?
- Do the listening selections include themes for score reading?
- Are there biographical sketches of composers and background information for musical selections?
- Are the words and music easy to read?
- Are the illustrations appropriate and attractive?
- Is the index so organized that various types of material can be located easily and quickly?

*1—excellent; 2—good; 3—fair; 4—unsatisfactory.

	*1	2	3	4

- Are the accompanying recordings of good quality?
- Is the teacher's guide complete and convenient to use?
- Does the teacher's guide contain sufficient background information regarding songs and listening selections?
- Are accompanying films, filmstrips, and books for student and teacher reference suggested?
- Will you *and* your students enjoy using this text in the classroom?

Appendix E:
Questions and Projects for Study
in College Classes

College classes in methodology may find the following study questions helpful. It is assumed that the instructor will demonstrate many of the lessons in each section and discuss procedures with the students before they undertake independent work.

The Music Class in the Junior High School

— What is the distinction between primary and secondary objectives?
— What are the advantages and disadvantages of existing scheduling patterns for the music class as found in the junior high schools?
— Observe the physical characteristics, attitudes, and reactions of the students in a junior high music class.
— Plan a panel discussion on the subject of teacher competencies.
— Write your own list of objectives for the first few days of a junior high music class.
— Select and teach (by the rote method) a song of the type suggested on page 17.

Singing

— Observe the voice testing procedure in a local school or invite junior high students into your class to demonstrate their vocal ranges and qualities.
— Select a song which fits the voice classifications in junior high and present it to the class.
— Discuss the advantages and disadvantages of several alternate seating plans.
— Teach a song for an assembly sing. Add instruments if possible.
— Arrange a simple folk song to fit unchanged, changing and changed voices.

MUSIC LISTENING

— What is the place of the listening program in a well-rounded junior high school music program?

— Suggest several ways in which the concept of student discovery may be applied to the listening program.

— Teach a listening lesson to the class involving singing and the use of instruments.

— Teach a listening lesson with a recording.

— Observe a listening lesson in a local school and write a report describing the procedure.

PLAYING INSTRUMENTS

— Select an appropriate jingle and add instruments as in the example on page 43.

— Create a rhythm chant and add instruments as in the example on pages 43 and 44.

— Write a lesson plan and teach a song with instrumental accompaniment.

UNDERSTANDING MELODY

— Discuss the structural characteristics of melody and write a procedure for teaching one or more of these characteristics.

— Write a lesson plan and teach a lesson on melodic setting to the class.

— Write a follow-up lesson on musical style using "Dances New and Dances Old" as a point of departure.

— Write a lesson plan for teaching a lesson on melodic composition in contemporary style.

UNDERSTANDING RHYTHM

— Select several musical examples appropriate for junior high school in which the element of rhythm is central.

— Write a lesson plan and teach one of the above to the class.

— Observe a lesson on rhythm in a local school and write a report describing the procedure.

— Write a lesson plan for teaching a lesson on contemporary rhythm.

UNDERSTANDING HARMONY

— Write a lesson plan and guide the class in a lesson on building basic chords.

— Arrange several types of keyboard accompaniments which junior high students would be able to play.

— Select a song having at least two horizontal harmony parts and teach it to the class. Be prepared to play the voice parts and accompaniment on the piano.

— Arrange an autoharp accompaniment to a unison or part song.

— Guide the class in creating a simple keyboard accompaniment to a familiar song.

Tone Color

— Plan and teach a lesson in which the increased appreciation of tone color is the primary objective.

— Select and arrange familiar melodies changing tone color with frequency as in example on p. 87.

— Add more examples to the list highlighting instruments of the orchestra.

Understanding Form

— Select several compositions which would clearly illustrate the principles of variety and unity.

— Write a lesson plan and teach one of the above to the class.

— Discuss the difference between form *in* music and forms *of* music.

— Prepare a lesson plan for teaching one of the following:
sonata-allegro, rondo, theme and variations, fugue.

Relating Content

— Prepare a lesson plan for a forty-minute lesson. Include objectives, activities, and development of the lesson.

— Prepare a unit on a musical topic and present one lesson from the unit to the class.

— Discuss the relationship between the objectives of the class and the teaching approach.

— Prepare a teaching lesson using materials found in "Ideas in a Nutshell."

Appendix F:
Recordings of Contemporary
Music for Classroom Use

Composer	Title	Recording
Antheil	Ballet Mecanique	Urania 134
Babbitt	Composition for Four Instruments	CRI 138
	Composition for Synthesizer	Col MS 6566
Bartók	Sonata for Two Pianos and Percussion	Col MS 6641
————	Music for Strings, Percussion, Celesta	Lon 6159
————	Two Portraits for Orchestra	Col MS 6789
Bouléz	Marteau sans Maitre	Odys 32160154
Britten	Peter Grimes: 4 Sea Interludes	Lon 6179
————	Serenade for Tenor, Horn, Strings	Lon 5358
Brubeck, H.	Dialogues for Jazz Combo and Orchestra	Col CS 8257
Burge	Eclipse II	Advance 3
Cage	Amores for Prepared Piano and Percussion	Time 58000
————	Variations	Col MS 7051
Carpenter	Skyscrapers	CBS 32110002
Chanler	Epitaphs	Col MS 6198
Chavez	Toccata for Percussion	Cap P-8299
Copland	Billy The Kid, Appalachian Spring	Col ML 5157
————	Connotations for Orchestra	(2) Col L2S-1008
————	Music for a Great City	CBS 32110002
Cowell	Homage to Iran	CRI 173
Creston	Two Chorus Dances	Cap P8245
————	Dance Overture	CRI 111
Crumb	Night Music I	CRI S-218
Dello Joio	Sonata No. 3 for Piano	Concert Disc. 1217
————	Epigraph	Desto (6) 416
Diamond	Rounds for String Orchestra	Cap P8245

Composer	Title	Recording
———	World of Paul Klee	CRI 140
Hanson	The Composer and His Orchestra	Mer 51075
———	Chorale and Alleluia	Mer 50084
Harris	Symphony No. 4	Van 2082
Harrison	Four Strict Songs for 8 Baritones and Orchestra	Louisville 58-2
Hindemith	Mathis der Maler	Col MS 6562
———	Trauermusik for Viola and Strings	Epic LC 3356
Honegger	Pacific 231 and Rugby	West 14486
Hovhaness	Mysterious Mountain	Vic LSC 2251
Imbrie	Legend for Orchestra	CRI 152
Ives	Fourth of July	Col MS 6889
———	Circus Band March	Van C-10013
———	Three Places in New England	Mer 90149
———	Symphony No. 1	Col MS 7111
Luening	Poem in Cycles and Bells, Tape Recorder and Orchestra	CRI 112
———	Gargoyles	Col MS 6566
McBride	Pumpkin Eater's Little Fugue	CRI 119
McKenzie	Introduction and Allegro for Percussion	Urania (5) 106
Mennin	Canzona for Band	Mer 50084
Milhaud	Les Choëphores	Col MS 6396
———	Saudades do Brazil	CR 22160114
Mossolov	Iron Foundry	Folk 6160
Piston	Symphony No. 4	Col ML 4992
———	Carnival Song	Fleetwood 6001
Prokofiev	Lieutenant Kiji Suite	Col MS 6545
Riegger	Dance Rhythm	CRI 117
Rogers, B.	Leaves from the Tale of Pinocchio	Desto (6) 424
———	Three Japanese Dances	Mer 90173
Schoenberg	Theme and Variations	Col MS 7041
———	Quartet No. 4	Col ML 4737
Schuller	Concertino for Jazz Quartet and Orchestra	Atlantic 1359
———	Seven Studies after Paul Klee	Vic LSC 2879
———	Densities I	Cam 802
Smith, H.	Contours for Orchestra	Louisville 632
Sowerby	All On a Summer's Day	Louisville 56-6
Stravinsky	Agon	Col MS 6022
———	Sacré du Printemps	Col MS 6010
———	Firebird	Col MS 6014

Composer	*Title*	*Recording*
Stockhausen	Gesang der Jüngelinge	DGG 13881
Toch	Geographical Fugue	Dec 10073
Ussachevsky	Sonic Contours	Folk 6160
————	Piece for Tape Recorder	CRI 112

Note: A recommended source for compositions and teaching suggestions: *Experiments in Musical Creativity*, Contemporary Music Project, Music Educators National Conference, Washington, D. C., 1966.

Appendix G:
Music Books
for the School Library

Anderson, Marian, *My Lord, What a Morning*. New York: Viking, 1956. (An autobiography.)

Apel, Willi, *Harvard Dictionary of Music*. Cambridge, Mass.: Harvard University Press, 1944.

———, and Ralph Daniel, *The Harvard Brief Dictionary of Music*. Cambridge, Mass.: Harvard University Press, 1960.

Atkinson, Margaret, and May Hillman, *Dancers of the Ballet*. New York: Knopf, 1955. (Biographies.)

Attaway, William, *Hear America Singing*; Intro. by Harry Belafonte. New York: Lion, 1968.

Bakeless, Katherine L., *Story Lives of Great Composers*, rev. ed. Philadelphia: Lippincott, 1953.

Balet, Jan, *What Makes an Orchestra*. New York: Oxford, 1951.

Barlow, Harold, and Sam Morgenstern, *Dictionary of Musical Themes*. New York: Crown, 1948.

Bernstein, Leonard, *The Joy of Music*. New York: Simon and Schuster, 1959.

———, *Young Peoples Concerts for Reading and Listening*. New York: Simon and Schuster, 1962. (Book and five 7-inch 33 1/3 recordings.)

Bernstein, Shirley, *Making Music: Leonard Bernstein*. Chicago: Encyclopaedia Brittanica, 1963.

Boni, Margaret, *Fireside Book of Folk Songs*. New York: Simon and Schuster, 1947.

Brand, Oscar, *Singing Holidays*. New York: Knopf, 1957.

Britten, Benjamin, and Imogen Holst, *Wonderful World of Music*. New York: Garden City, 1958.

Browne, Charles A., rev. by Willard Heaps, *The Story of Our National Ballads*. New York: Crowell, 1960.

Buchanan, Fannie, and Charles Luckenbill, *How Man Made Music*, rev. ed., Chicago: Follett, 1959.

Bulla, Clyde, *Stories of Favorite Operas*. New York: Crowell, 1959.

Burch, Gladys, *Famous Pianists for Boys and Girls*. New York: Dodd, Mead, 1956.

———, *Famous Violinists for Young People*. New York: Dodd, Mead, 1946.

Chissell, Joan, *Chopin*. New York: Crowell, 1965.
Cross, Milton, *New Complete Stories of Great Operas*, rev. ed. New York: Doubleday, 1955.
Cross, Milton John, and David Ewen, *Encyclopedia of the Great Composers and Their Music*, new rev. ed. New York: Doubleday, 1962.
Cunningham, Dale, *Picture Book of Music and Its Makers*. New York: Sterling, 1963.
Davis, Marilyn, and Arnold Broido, *Music Dictionary*, rev. ed. New York: Doubleday, 1956.
Day, Lillian. *Paganini*. London: Hyperion, 1946.
Deucher, Sybil, *Edvard Grieg, Boy of the Northland*. New York: Dutton, 1946.
Dietz, Betty, and Michael Olatunji, *Musical Instruments of Africa* (with 7-inch record). New York: John Day, 1965.
Eaton, Jeanette, *Trumpeter's Tale*. New York: Morrow, 1955. (The story of Louis Armstrong.)
Erlich, Lillian, *What Is Jazz All About?* New York: Messner, 1962.
Ewen, David, *Encyclopedia of Concert Music*. New York: Hill and Wang, 1959.
————, *The Story of Jerome Kern*. New York: Holt, 1953.
————, *The Story of Arturo Toscanini*, rev. ed. New York: Holt, 1960.
————, *A Journey into Greatness: The Life and Music of George Gershwin*. New York: Holt, 1956.
————, *The Story of Irving Berlin*. New York: Holt, 1950.
————, *Tales from the Vienna Woods*. New York: Holt, 1944.
————, *The World of Jerome Kern*. New York: Holt, 1960.
————, *Famous Instrumentalists*. New York: Dodd, Mead, 1965.
————, *Leonard Bernstein: A Biography for Young People*. Philadelphia: Chilton, 1965.
————, *With a Song in his Heart* (Story of Richard Rodgers). New York: Holt, 1963.
Fox, Lilla M., *Instruments of Popular Music*. New York: Roy, 1968.
Gollomb, Joseph, *Albert Schweitzer, Genius of the Jungle*. New York: Vanguard, 1949.
Goss, Madeleine, and Robert Schauffler, *Brahms, the Master*. New York: Holt, 1943.
Gough, Catherine, *Boyhoods of Great Composers*. Books 1 and 2. New York: Walck, 1961, 1965.
Goulden, Shirley, *Royal Book of Ballet*. Chicago: Follett, 1962.
Graham, Alberta, *Great Bands of America*. New York: Nelson, 1951.
Heaps, Willard A., and Porter W. Heaps, *Singing Sixties*. Norman, Oklahoma: University of Oklahoma Press, 1960. (Civil War songs.)
Hentoff, Nat, *Jazz Country*. New York: Harper & Row, 1965.
Higgins, Helen, *Stephen Foster, Boy Minstrel*. Indianapolis: Bobbs, Merrill, 1953.
Hill, Lorna, *Dream of Sadler's Wells*. New York: Holt, 1955. (Ballet.)
Hughes, Langston, *Famous Negro Music Makers*. New York: Dodd, Mead, 1955.
————, *First Book of Jazz*. New York: Watts, 1955.
Huntington, Harriet E., *Tune Up*: The Instruments of the Orchestra and Their Players. New York: Doubleday, 1942.

Hyatt, Malcolm, and Walter Fabell, comp., *Gilbert and Sullivan Song Book.* New York: Random House, 1955.

Irving, Robert, *Sound and Ultrasonics.* New York: Knopf, 1959.

Kauffman, *The Story of Haydn.* New York: Grossett and Dunlap, 1962.

Keepnews, Orrin, and Bill Grauer, *Pictorial History of Jazz.* New York: Crown, 1955.

Kellogg, Charlotte H., *Paderewski.* New York: Viking, 1956.

Kert, Russell, and Deems Taylor (compiled by Rupert Hughes), *Music Lovers' Encyclopedia.* New York: Garden City, 1954.

Kielty, Bernardine, *Jenny Lind Sang Here.* Boston: Houghton Mifflin, 1959.

Lingg, Ann M., *John Philip Sousa.* New York: Holt, 1954.

Machlis, Joseph, *American Composers of Our Time.* New York: Crowell, 1963.

Malvern, Gladys, *Dancing Star,* new ed. New York: Collins, 1952. (The life of Pavlova.)

Mara, Thalia, and Lee Wyndham, *First Steps in Ballet.* New York: Garden City, 1955.

Maynard, Olga, *The Ballet Companion.* Philadelphia: Macrae Smith, 1957.

Menotti, Gian-Carlo, *Amahl and the Night Visitors.* New York: McGraw-Hill, 1952.

Mirsky, Reba Paeff, *Johann Sebastian Bach.* Chicago: Follett, 1965.

———, *Beethoven.* Chicago: Follett, 1957.

———, *Haydn.* Chicago: Follett, 1963.

———, *Mozart.* Chicago: Follett, 1960.

Pauli, Hertha, *Silent Night, The Story of a Song.* New York: Knopf, 1951.

Posell, Elsa, *American Composers.* Boston: Houghton Mifflin, 1963.

———, *This Is an Orchestra.* Boston: Houghton Mifflin, 1950. (Story about the orchestra.)

Power-Waters, Alma S., *Melody Maker.* New York: Dutton, 1959. (The life of Sir Arthur Sullivan.)

Purdy, Claire Lee, *He Heard America Sing.* New York: Messner, 1940. (The life of Stephen Foster.)

———, *Song of the North.* New York: Messner, 1943. (The life of Grieg.)

———, *Stormy Victory.* New York: Messner, 1942. (The life of Tchaikovsky.)

Sandburg, Carl, ed., *The New American Songbag.* New York: Associated Music, 1950.

Sandved, K. B., *et al.,* eds., *The World of Music.* London: Waverly Book Company, 1954.

Scholes, Percy, *Oxford Junior Companion to Music.* London: Oxford University Press, 1954.

Siegmeister, Elie, *Invitation to Music.* Irvington-on-Hudson, N. Y.: Harvey House, 1961. (Record—*Invitation to Music,* Folkways FT 3603.)

Shippen, Katherine, and Anca Seidlova, *The Heritage of Music.* New York: Viking, 1963.

Skolsky, Syd, *Music Box Book.* New York: Dutton, 1946.

Slonimsky, Nicholas, *The Road to Music,* rev. ed. New York: Dodd, Mead, 1966.

Stoddard, Hope, *From These Come Music.* New York: Crowell, 1962.

Terkel, Studs, *Giants of Jazz.* New York: Crowell, 1957.

Thomas, Henry, and Dana Lee Thomas, *Living Biographies of Great Composers.* New York: Garden City, 1959.

Trapp, Maria, *The Story of the Trapp Family Singers*. Philadelphia: Lippincott, 1949.

Ulanov, Barry, *Handbook of Jazz*. New York: Viking, 1957.

Ulrich, Homer, *Famous Women Singers*. New York: Dodd, Mead, 1956.

Wheeler, Opal, *Adventures of Richard Wagner*. New York: Dutton, 1960.

————, *Peter Tchaikovsky and the Nutcracker Ballet*. New York: Dutton, 1959.

————, *H. M. S. Pinafore*. New York: Dutton, 1946. (Story and music.)

————, *Sing for America*. New York: Dutton, 1944.

————, *Sing for Christmas*. New York: Dutton, 1943.

White, Hilda, *Song Without End*. New York: Dutton, 1959. (The love story of the Schumanns.)

Woody, Regina, *Dancing for Joy*. New York: Dutton, 1959.

Bibliography

Andrews, Frances M., and Joseph A. Leeder, *Guiding Junior-High-School Pupils in Music Experiences.* Englewood Cliffs, N. J.: Prentice-Hall, 1953.

Baldwin, Lillian, *Music to Remember.* Morristown, N. J.: Silver-Burdett, 1951.

Bernstein, Leonard, *The Joy of Music.* New York: Simon and Schuster, 1959.

Bruner, Jerome, *Process of Education.* Cambridge: Harvard University Press, 1960.

Burrows, Raymond, and Bessie Redmond, comp., *Symphony Themes.* New York: Simon and Schuster, 1942.

Conant, James B., *Education in the Junior High School Years.* Los Angeles, California: Educational Testing Service, 1960.

Copland, Aaron, *What to Listen for in Music.* New York: McGraw-Hill, 1939.

Experiments in Musical Creativity, Contemporary Music Project, Washington, D.C.: Music Educators National Conference, 1966.

Frandsen, Arden N., *Educational Psychology.* New York: McGraw-Hill, 1961.

Function of Music in the Secondary School Curriculum. Washington, D.C.: Music Educators National Conference, 1952.

Gehrkens, Karl W., *Music in the Junior High School.* Evanston, Ill.: Summy-Birchard, 1936.

Hartshorn, William C., *Music for the Academically Talented Student.* Washington, D.C.: Music Educators National Conference, 1960.

Hartshorn, William C., and Helen S. Leavitt, *The Pilot; The Mentor.* Boston: Ginn, 1940.

Hoffer, Charles, *Teaching Music in the Secondary Schools.* Belmont, California: Wadsworth, 1964.

Hood, Marguerite V., and E. J. Schultz, *Learning Music Through Rhythm.* Boston: Ginn, 1949.

Howard, John Tasker, and James Lyon, *Modern Music.* New York: Crowell, 1957.

Hughes, William, *Planning for Junior High School Music.* Belmont, California: Wadsworth, 1967.

Karel, Leon C., *Avenues to the Arts.* Kirksville, Missouri: Simpson, 1966.

Leonhard, Charles, and Robert W. House, *Foundations and Principles of Music Education.* New York: McGraw-Hill, 1959.

Lindgren, Henry C., *Educational Psychology in the Classroom.* New York: Wiley, 1956.

Machlis, Joseph, *Introduction to Contemporary Music*. New York: Norton, 1961.

Manlove, Donald C., and David W. Beggs III, *Bold New Ventures*. Bloomington, Indiana: Indiana University Press, 1965.

Miller, William H., *Introduction to Music Appreciation*. Philadelphia: Chilton, 1961.

Monsour, Sally, Marilyn Cohen, and Patricia Lindell, *Rhythm in Music and Dance for Children*. Belmont, California: Wadsworth, 1966.

Mursell, James L., *Music Education Principles and Programs*. Morristown, N. J.: Silver-Burdett, 1956.

Music Buildings, Rooms and Equipment, Bulletin #17. Washington, D.C.: Music Educators National Conference, 1956.

Music Curriculum in Secondary Schools. Washington, D.C.: Music Educators National Conference, 1959.

Nordholm, Harriett, and Ruth Bakewell, *Keys to Teaching Junior High School Music*. Minneapolis: Schmitt, Hall & McCreary, 1953.

Pitts, Lilla Belle, *The Music Curriculum in a Changing World*. Morristown, N. J.: Silver-Burdett, 1944.

Romine, Stephen A., *Building the High School Curriculum*. New York: Ronald Press, 1954.

Rorke, Genevieve, *Choral Teaching at the Junior High School Level*. Minneapolis: Schmitt, Hall & McCreary, 1947.

Rosewall, Richard B., *Handbook of Singing*. Evanston, Ill.: Summy-Birchard, 1961.

Singleton, Ira, *Music in Secondary School*. Boston: Allyn and Bacon, 1963.

Smith, Henry P., *Psychology in Teaching*, 2nd ed. Englewood Cliffs, N. J.: Prentice-Hall, 1962.

Stringham, Edward J., *Listening to Music Creatively*, 2nd ed. Englewood Cliffs, N. J.: Prentice-Hall, 1959.

Sur, William R., and Charles F. Schuller, *Music Education for Teen-agers*. New York: Harper and Row, 1958.

Thelen, Herbert A., *Education and the Human Quest*. New York: Harper and Row, 1960.

Tooze, Ruth, and Beatrice P. Krone, *Literature and Music as Resources for Social Studies*. Englewood Cliffs, N. J.: Prentice-Hall, 1955.

Wilson, A. Verne, *Design for Musical Understanding*. Evanston, Illinois: Summy-Birchard, 1966.

Indexes

Index of Musical Examples

Subject Index